10 Ø

4

Ocean Flying

McGRAW-HILL SERIES IN AVIATION

David B. Thurston Consulting Editor

Ocean Flying

Louise Sacchi
President, Sacchi Air Ferry Enterprises

McGraw-Hill Book Company

New York   St. Louis   San Francisco   Auckland
Bogotá   Düsseldorf   Johannesburg   London
Madrid   Mexico   Montreal   New Delhi
Panama   São Paulo   Singapore
Sydney   Tokyo   Toronto

Library of Congress Cataloging in Publication Data

Sacchi, Louise.
  Ocean flying.

  Includes index.
  1. Overwater flying.   I.   Title.
TL711.026S22   629.132'5'09162   78-31976
ISBN 0-07-054405-0

1234567890 BPBP   7865432109

*The editors for this book were Jeremy Robinson and Margaret Lamb,
the designer was Naomi Auerbach, and the production supervisor
was Teresa F. Leaden. It was set in Electra by
Progressive Typographers.*

Printed and bound by The Book Press.

DEDICATED with Gratitude

To

Marion, with whom I first crossed the North Atlantic

Lucille, who has always interceded and helped in every possible way.

Fred, Don, and Hutch, who encouraged the formation of S.A.F.E.

Wiggins, Butler, and Atlantic personnel, who always went all out to assist me

Weather, Customs, and Air Control people, whose interest and cooperation did so much to make my trips pleasant

Bob and Walt, who gave generously of their route knowledge

The Beech distributors around the world (now my friends), without whose airplanes there could have been no S.A.F.E.

Contents

Preface

Breathes there a Pilot with soul so dead
Who never to himself has said:
"I really wish that I could flee
In my own plane across the Sea."
  With apologies to Sir Walter Scott!

B ecause there is some of Walter Mitty in all of us, more
and more pilots are dreaming of such an adventure.
This book is written for those pilots.

Aircraft ownership is not a prerequisite for realizing the
dream, but it does remove one obstacle. My dreaming began in 1940, but it was 1962 before it became reality.

Sometimes a dream is better than the reality when it
comes; for me the reality was all I had hoped for and more.
It so remains after 333 crossings of Atlantic and Pacific
delivering airplanes to countries in all quarters of the globe.

The Oceans are vast, powerful, temperamental, and de-
manding of respect, as any sailor can tell you. Therefore
some knowledge of Ocean and Weather, Airplane and
Engine, and Navigation and Self is essential to success.

In the following pages I shall share with you the knowledge I have gained in those 333 crossings in General Avia-

tion airplanes, both single- and twin-engine, piston engine and turbo-prop.

One never stops learning, and I make no pretense of knowing all there is to know in this area. However, the information in this book, if utilized, will enable you to make your dream come true with safety and pleasure, as I have done so often.

Aviation Language

L ike that of any profession or specialized occupation, the language of aviation sounds to the passenger or nonpilot rather like the Tower of Babel. When we start flying internationally there are new words and phrases, even for the experienced domestic pilot. The new and the not-so-new are listed here for convenience and used for simplicity in the text.

ADF (Automatic Direction Finder): The low medium-frequency radio receiver in the airplane. The needle on the indicator points to the transmitting station.

ADIZ (Air Defense Identification Zone): This may be coastal, offshore, or inland. On an ocean flight it is a required reporting point.

AIS (Airport Information Service): This is somewhat similar to our FSS, in that it is the place where we file flight plans and request information. Weather information is not found here, however.

AIRPORT COMPASS ROSE: A type of circle with lines pointing to the magnetic points of the compass; it is found on a portion of the airport which is free of any magnetic disturbance (at least we hope it is!).

ALTERNATE AIRPORT: A place to go if the weather at destination turns sour. On a transoceanic flight it can be problematical.

ANOXIA: Oxygen deprivation or deficiency, as from high-altitude flying in a nonpressurized plane.

BEARING: The direction of one object from another. It comes in several models, including:
Relative: measured from the nose of the airplane
True: measured from True North
Magnetic: measured from Magnetic North

BFO (Beat Frequency Oscillator): An addition to the circuitry of the ADF which enables the pilot to identify a station having an A/2 emission, as is common in Europe, Africa, and Asia.

CAVOK (Ceiling and Visibility OK): A phrase found in weather reports and forecasts in other countries when the ceiling is 5000 feet or more and the visibility is 6 nautical miles (10 kilometers) or more.

CELSIUS: Temperature scale divided into 100 parts between freezing and boiling (formerly called centigrade). Anders Celsius was the Swedish astronomer who first described this method of measuring temperature.

CONSOL: An extinct method of oceanic navigation by means of dots and dashes; some of the stations are still listed on the charts though no longer in operation.

COURSE: A line drawn on a chart between two points. On an Aircraft Position Chart it is a *True* Course; on a Radio Facility Chart it is a Magnetic Course.

DME (Distance Measuring Equipment): A black box in the airplane which tells your distance from a VORTAC or VOR/DME station.

DOPPLER: A sophisticated system of navigation used in the higher altitudes.

ETA: Estimated time of arrival.

ETD: Estimated time of departure.

ETE: Estimated time enroute.

EQUI-TIME POINT: The place at which the time to return to where you came from is the same as the time to continue to your destination.

FIR (Flight Information Region): The dividing line between two FIRs (or control areas) is a compulsory reporting point on an international flight plan.

FL (Flight Level): Term used for altitude when using standard altimeter setting of 1013.2 millibars or 29.92 inches of mercury. This also comes in various models:
> *Domestic:* above 18,000 feet
> *Oceanic:* any altitude after leaving the coast
> *Foreign:* any altitude above the transition level, which will be given by the Controller at departure and when approaching destination

GMT (Greenwich Mean Time): Standard time for all navigation, it originates at Greenwich, England; also known as Zulu time.

GROUND CUSHION: The air which is compressed between the ground and the wing when the wing is from one-half to seven-eighths of its span above the ground or water.

HEADING: The direction in which the airplane is pointed:
> *True:* when related to *True* North
> *Magnetic:* when related to Magnetic North

HF (High Frequency Radio): Communications radio which operates on the higher-frequency band for really long distance transmission and reception.

ICAO (International Civil Aviation Organization): An organization of aviation departments of all the countries who make rules and regulations for international use of the air.

IFR (Instrument Flight Rules): The method of flying when you cannot see the ground.

IMC (Instrument Meteorological Conditions): A term used in other countries to denote bad weather.

INS (Inertial Navigation System): A very sophisticated and expensive method of push-button navigation.

JET STREAM: A fast-moving river of high-altitude air which usually moves South in the winter and North in the summer (like some people I know).

KILOMETER: The coming method of distance measurement; designed to confuse all English-speaking peoples, it is 0.54 nautical mile. Used for visibility in Europe and Asia.

KNOT: A unit of speed equal to 1 nautical mile per hour. Used universally and found on most modern airspeed indicators.

LATITUDE: Distance North or South of the equator, measured in degrees, minutes, and seconds; 1 minute of latitude equals 1 nautical mile.

LONGITUDE: Distance East or West of the Prime Meridian at Greenwich, England. The International Date Line is the 180th meridian.

LOP (Line of Position): A line drawn on the chart from a radio bearing or a celestial body. You are somewhere on this line, and if you can get another LOP to intersect with the first, their crossing is your position.

LORAN (Longe Range Navigation): A time-differential method of navigation for ships and aircraft and simple enough for small aircraft. When the aircraft is in precipitation, the image on the oscilloscope looks like grass and becomes useless with Loran A. Loran C is better in such conditions.

MAGNETIC POLES: Large magnetic fields which attract the Magnetic Compass in airplanes or ships. Their approximate positions in 1975:

North: 76°N100°W on Bathurst Island

South: 69°S139°E on Antarctic continent

MILLIBARS: Metric method of measuring atmospheric pressure; 1013.2 millibars = 29.92 inches of mercury, which is sea-level standard pressure. A millibar is defined as 1000 dynes per square centimeter, or 100 pascals in the International System (SI).

NAUTICAL MILE: Unit of distance in universal navigational use. One nautical mile equals one minute of latitude as measured up and down a meridian of longitude.

NDB (Non-Directional Beacon): A low-frequency radio transmitter whose signal is non-directional, that is, is emitted in all directions.

OAT (Outside Air Temperature): The free-air temperature which is essential for correction of airspeed and altimeter readings and for indicating the possibility of icing conditions.

OCTARE: One-eighth of the sky, the unit of measure used in foreign countries for the amount of cloud cover.

OCA (Oceanic Control Area): The line between two OCAs is the same as the dividing line of the FIRs and is a compulsory reporting point.

OMEGA: A method of long-range navigation.

PROG CHART (Prognostic Chart): The significant weather or upper-wind chart which is interpolated from available data by the computer.

ONC (Operational Navigation Charts): These charts have the same 1:1,000,000 as our WACs of the United States, but they cover twice the territory so are not so convenient in the cockpit.

QFE: One of the International Q code symbols which indicates the atmospheric pressure at the airport elevation.

QNH: The international Q code symbol which indicates sea-level atmospheric pressure, or what we call altimeter setting.

RADAR ALTIMETER: An electronic device which measures the time for a radio signal to go from aircraft to ground or water and back, thereby giving an accurate altitude without regard to the atmospheric pressure.

RADIAL: The magnetic course *outbound* from either a VOR or an NDB. To proceed toward the station it is necessary to fly the reciprocal.

RADIO FACILITY CHART: One which deals almost exclusively with radio aids and airways and has very little topographical information. The charts are printed separately for high-altitude airways and low-altitude airways.

RMI (Radio Magnetic Indicator): A navigation instrument which takes its heading information from a slaved gyro and whose two needles are tied into the VOR and ADF receivers to provide bearings to the stations.

SAY AGAIN, YOU'RE BROKEN: A very useful phrase for those occasions when you have no idea what the man said and suspect he was not speaking English.

SAY AGAIN, YOU WERE CUT OUT: Another way of saying the same thing.

STAND-BY: Useful when asked a question to which you do not have the answer; this gives you time to think.

TACAN (TACtical Air Navigation): A military navigation system which will give distance if your DME receiver is tuned to the correct channel. See Appendix C for list of receiving channels.

TAFOR (Terminal Area FORecast): The initials used as a word when requesting forecasts in other countries.

TCA (Terminal Control Area): The upside-down wedding cake of air over busy airports in the United States; also the airspace of varying shapes over foreign airports.

TRANSITION LEVEL: The altitude at which you change from local pressure to standard pressure; reporting changes from "altitude" to "flight level."

UNABLE: The answer to give when the controller wants you to climb higher than you think wise, or he wants to send you into a black cloud, or tells you to call on a frequency requiring 90 to 100 turns of your trailing antenna and your arm hurts!

USEFUL LOAD: The difference between the empty weight of the airplane and its gross weight.

VERIFY: Means "Do you really mean what I think you mean?" If the controller asks you to verify your estimate, you had better figure it again. If you are uncertain about a frequency, "verify" will get it for you without having to admit ignorance.

VLF (Very Low Frequency): Another method of navigation.

VFR (Visual Flight Rules): Navigating with constant reference to the ground.

VHF (Very High Frequency): Line-of-sight radio transmission and reception.

VOR: Very high frequency Omni-directional Range.

WEATHER FOLDER: A complete weather briefing in the form of maps and teletype information which is put into a folder for your flight.

WHAT AM I DOING HERE?: The question you will ask yourself at certain times when things get wormy.

ZONE: In transocean flying it is the area between the 5 degree meridians of longitude counting from 1 to 36 as we proceed West from Greenwich to the International Date Line, starting with 1 to 36 from there on around to Greenwich again.

ZULU TIME: A term dreamed up by the military which is easier to say than Greenwich Mean Time; in writing it is shortened to Z (0935Z).

Ocean Flying

1 An Airplane and Its Crew

S he is built like a bird with wings spread for soaring; her
swallow tail is designed for speed and beauty (Figure
1-1). Her flight attitude can be changed in any direction
with a finger touch on her controls through the cables and
rods which are her nerve system. Her motive power is a 285-
horsepower engine mounted in her nicely shaped nose.
Its fuel is stored in her wings, also in the cabin area for this
delivery flight. All but the left front seat have been removed
and folded into the baggage compartment, to be replaced
with two 60-gallon tanks.

Her brain manifests itself in those faces on the instrument panel; the instruments which tell of engine health, attitude in space, and our speed and direction of flight over
this watery expanse of the North Atlantic.

On this sunny Sunday afternoon, in grace and beauty she
floats just above a sea of whipped-cream clouds, some of
them standing in little peaks. Her companion shadow on

the clouds is surrounded by a bright rainbow, and 9000 feet below but quite unseen lie the cold ocean waters.

In that left front seat is the crew—pilot, copilot, navigator, and flight engineer—the crew which is directing her path from her birthplace in the United States to her new

FIGURE 1-1
The beautiful swallowtail Bonanza in flight.

home somewhere in Europe. The seat is not as crowded as it sounds because pilot, copilot, navigator, and engineer are all wrapped in one skin—mine.

My navigator's hat makes me the busiest member of this crew. Before we departed from Gander, Newfoundland, very early this morning I had spent some time with the meteorologist in the Weather Office studying the "Prog" charts and the satellite pictures to determine the possible weather enroute. We also compared the very few actual upper winds available for the 700-millibar (10,000-foot) level with the forecast winds. These winds and their accuracy are important to our estimated time enroute and fuel reserve.

I decided that today's would be a good flight as there are

no weather systems over the ocean, and I believe the forecast that the wind will be almost a tailwind.

After this careful briefing, and clutching my weather folder, I adjourned, as always, to the cafeteria for breakfast and flight planning. With my coffee is the time to work out a wind triangle on the computer for each of the nine zones (a zone is 5 degrees of longitude) across to Shannon. These will give me the *True* Heading and groundspeed for each zone because they are based on the *True* Course taken from the chart and the *True* upper winds. I add the Westerly Variation to get a Magnetic Heading and figure the time enroute for each zone.

Also needed is an equi-time point, which is the point midway in time between returning to Gander and continuing to Shannon; beyond that point if I have any trouble, I am closer to Shannon than to Gander in time. The ICAO or International Flight Plan Form requires that I enter the actual time of departure and actual time over each reporting point in GMT or Zulu. I add up the time I will need before takeoff; 20 minutes to go up to Air Traffic Control to fill out the ICAO flight plan, 15 minutes to find the Airport Attendant and pay the airport fees, 5 minutes for the last "pit stop," 15 minutes to get out to the airplane and do a careful preflight check. Newfoundland's Atlantic Time is $3^{1}/_{2}$ hours behind GMT, so their Daylight Saving Time is $2^{1}/_{2}$ hours behind. It is now 0630 local, so that is 0900 GMT and I should be ready to go at 0955 GMT (Zulu). Allowing 5 minutes for an approach at Shannon gives an estimated time of arrival of 1900 GMT on the 24-hour clock.

Even though I had swung the compass myself at Wiggins after the tanks and the HF radio and Loran were installed, I pause briefly on Runway 9 to check the compass again. Now that we are airborne, I work a Loran fix from two stations about every 20 minutes to be sure that the heading and groundspeed are still as filed and, if necessary, correct any change in drift angle. I also tune the ADF to any shore station within its range and check the bearing against my

Loran fix. I can usually receive the BBC station at Birmingham in England on 200 kilohertz from about 40° West, and Athlone in Ireland on 565.5 kilohertz from about 25° West.

Most of my work as flight engineer has already been done. Coming up from Boston, I ran the engine for a time out of each ferry tank so I know that both are feeding properly. Before we left Gander this morning, I drained fuel from each tank and the strainer into my plastic drainer to be sure there was no fuzz or other dirt, rechecked the oil level, and looked around under the cowling for birds' nests or other foreign bodies, and everything is OK. I removed the pitot cover, put the chocks in the baggage compartment, and walked around the airplane looking for discrepancies. When I opened the cabin door, I sniffed for fumes from the cabin tanks because fuel fumes give me a bad headache; there were no fumes or smell, but I forgot to look at the cabin tank vent on the belly. If it clogs, the tanks will not feed properly, but it was open and free; while I was down underneath, I made sure that the funnel and weight of the HF antenna was not jammed in the tube. It can be very embarrassing if the antenna won't reel out, because then there is nothing you can do about it, and of course neither the HF or the Loran will work. It happened to me once, and then several years later I got careless again and once more I had no HF or Loran.

Now that we are airborne and I have done what I could to ensure that the airplane and engine will not spring any unpleasant surprises, I will monitor the engine instruments and watch and time the tanks, particularly the ones in the cabin, which have no gages. The engine-driven fuel pump on this engine pumps 22 gallons per hour at 63 percent power of which the engine is using 13^1/$_2$ gallons, so the other 8^1/$_2$ gallons goes back into whichever wing tank is being used. However, the cabin tanks have been tied in so that when they are in use, the extra fuel goes into the right wing, which means that I must use the fuel from the right wing first to leave room; otherwise I will be pumping fuel overboard, and this would shorten my range more than a little.

I try to switch tanks at the last minute to use all the fuel available, but without letting the engine cough; this always gives the crew an unwanted shot of adrenalin.

Because its new owner ordered an autopilot as well as all the other goodies one could want, this is an extremely well-equipped single-engine airplane. Once the pilot and copilot have made the takeoff and climb, with care to gain and keep a little extra speed because we are 10 percent over gross, I have as little to do as the pilot and first officer of any airliner overhead. Every 5 degrees of longitude, which my flight plan estimated to be approximately every hour, one of me will make a position report.

"Gander, Gander, Gander—Sacchi 252—position."

Depending on atmospheric conditions, the number of frequencies in use, and other traffic, this may take several calls interspaced with periods of listening before I hear:

"Sacchi 252, this is Gander; go ahead your position."

"Sacchi 252—position five two three zero North, three five West at one three zero five, flight level nine zero. Estimate five three North, three zero West at one four zero five; on top. Copy Shanwick." (This is the standard format for a position report.)

"Sacchi 252, Gander copies your position five two three zero North, three five West at one three zero five, flight level nine zero. Estimate five three North, three zero West at one four zero five; on top. Copy Shanwick. Is that Charlie?"

"Sacchi 252—that is Charlie."

"OK, 252—at three zero West contact Shanwick. Have a good trip."

"Thanks, see you next week."

This exchange may go fast and smoothly, or it may take up to 15 minutes because of static and/or interference from other traffic. There are also times for all of us, whether airline, military, or civilian, when we cannot get through at all from our position because of sunspots or precipitation static or equipment failure. Then we must request a relay from some other airplane which may be in a better position. We switch to the emergency frequency which must be monitored by all aircraft crossing the ocean, and say:

"Does any aircraft read Sacchi 252 on one two one decimal five?"

Somebody will answer: "This is _____ 55, what can I do for you!"

It may be that two or even three or more answers will come, so pick the clearest.

"_____ 55, will you switch to one two three four five and relay to Gander for me, please?" When you are both on the frequency 123.45, give him the position report. He will read it back to you, and in a few minutes will either tell you that Gander has received it or that he could not get through either—at which point you will hope for better luck next time.

Even with the duties of four crew members combined in one person, today there is still time to enjoy the warmth of the sun, and wonder idly about the origin and destination of the airliners drawing the myriad contrails overhead. At this time of day, they are all Westbound because all airlines of whatever nationality schedule their departures from the European side at the same time, compete for altitudes and routes across the ocean, and arrive in the United States at the same time, thus ensuring congestion at all airports on both sides. In the middle of the night, everybody is Eastbound. Occasionally I talk to one going against the tide, but he is usually a cargo flight.

The contrails today make an almost braided pattern as they drift across each other with the wind; occasionally the sun flashes on one of the high flying jets drawing them. It is a beautiful sight and I take a picture of one passing right over me (Figure 1-2).

It was different on the last trip. The weather was fairly bad, so the Loran was unreadable in the precipitation; the

HF radio was useless because of precipitation static. Relays were necessary for several position reports, and there was no autopilot to ease the load; that time the crew was really busy. Oh well, that kind of trip makes me appreciate this one even more.

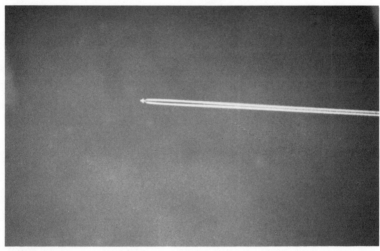

FIGURE 1-2

Nine thousand feet Eastbound looking at thirty-five thousand Westbound.

With two communication radios, I am monitoring not only the emergency frequency but also the commonly used conversational frequency of 123.45. Eavesdropping can be very interesting. Often I hear one airliner requesting a relay from another or one telling another that Gander or Shanwick is looking for him. Airline competition for business does not extend to the flight crews over the ocean; all are helpful to each other, to the military, and to us down in the lower levels of the sky.

Sometimes the conversations have a different twist and like the old *Perils of Pauline* movies leave you wondering. This conversation is an example of what I mean.

"_____ 601, this is 361—do you read?"

"361 from 601, go ahead."

"How far ahead of me are you? I've been trying to get

thirty-seven from Shanwick, but they say you are my traffic. What kind of wind have you at thirty-five?"

"We are about two minutes ahead of you and we have a minus forty on the wind."

"OK, guess we will have to wait a while for higher; hope not too long as we have a minus sixty at thirty three and are burning too much fuel down here at Mach eight. Say, did you hear about Joe? He will be grounded a long time I understand."

"Yeah, I heard; I guess he will be more careful next time."

"I'll bet."

What did Joe do—or have done to him—to ground him for a long time?

One night I quickly got out pencil and paper, because two airline crews were trading information on eating places in London. Some of them were very good indeed, but I had not known about them before. Then there was the day I learned about the charter airline which was laying off crews, and one of the second officers asked me for a job.

Several times it has happened that when I was talking to an airliner, either to request a relay or just for conversation, I'd hear:

"Louise, is that you? This is Peter" (or Walter or Henri, etc.).

These are usually pilots of foreign air carriers whom I have come to know in the course of return trips with them; sometimes they are other ferry pilots I have met at various airports around the world. These conversations can become a round robin with as many as five or six voices joining in. The question that always produces gasps from the airline types when I answer is "What are you flying today?"

"A single-engine Bonanza [or whatever]."

Life is seldom dull on the North Atlantic! It is not like the Pacific, where traffic is very light and you fly seemingly for hours with no conversation and usually nothing challenging about the weather, so sometimes you begin to wonder if you are still in the world. Out there, if you see a contrail, you immediately try to make contact just to talk to somebody.

Now the frequencies are quiet for some minutes, and I am hungry; it is time to dig out my implements and food and have a snack. If I don't eat every 3 or 4 hours, I get a headache. On this trip I have a can of Boston brown bread and a package of cream cheese, some bananas, and my bottle of water.

After eating I work another Loran fix to check my 30° West position; then report it to both Gander and Shanwick; 30° West is the beginning of Shanwick's control area and search area.

By 23° West the undercast has dissipated and there are only a few puffy cumulus clouds left. The sea underneath is as blue as the sky above, and I think how very fortunate I am to be flying a beautiful new and well-equipped airplane across an ocean as friendly as it is today. My mind begins to wander back in time to the events leading up to today. The flight instruction, the charter flying and corporate flying, all the years of trying to persuade some ferry company to hire me and being refused because of my sex. This made it necessary to form my own ferry company, which has turned out well.

Ooops! I forgot to change tanks; glad this is a Continental engine which is much more ladylike in announcing its imminent starvation than a Lycoming, which will stop abruptly. This one coughs first, so I move fast to switch the tank and turn on the electric boost pump to eliminate any air bubble.

Anyway, it is time to stop daydreaming and give Shanwick my 20° West position report. At 20° West, Shanwick always tells you to report 15° West on VHF, even though we tell them that at 9000 feet we are still too far out for VHF communication. After all, 15° West is 200 nautical miles out and VHF is line-of-sight.

About 10 peaceful minutes after this position report, my thoughts are interrupted by something vaguely seen from the corner of my right eye. I turn to look and see a *head* on my right wing tip. Fortunately the autopilot is doing the flying, because I really jump. Another look confirms that there is indeed a head on the wing tip, enclosed in a canopy although it is so close that I cannot see any other part of an airplane. I wave at the head rather tentatively, but get only a stare in response. Then the head moves back—my goodness—and I realize that it is a Harrier, the RAF vertical-takeoff fighter which can fly in any direction. He backs away and circles around me, coming again to rest on my right wing tip. Now he lifts his hand, so I show him my mike and try all the frequencies I have without success. I content myself with waving again, and this time he waves back and even smiles.

Again he backs away, circles around me, and pulls up in front in a spectacular half-roll; then dives for the sea. As my eyes follow his descent, I discover that there is an aircraft carrier down there along with several other warship types. It must be some sort of war game that I have stumbled over all unsuspecting; I suppose he was sent up to see whether I was an enemy spy, or maybe he just wanted to see if he could startle me. He could!

Why, oh why, didn't I reload my camera after that last shot of the contrail? Nobody will believe such a story without a picture to prove it.

At 15° West, I call Shanwick again on the HF radio, give my position report, and assure them that I will contact Shannon on VHF as soon as I can. This will be at 13° West, which is about 150 nautical miles out. In another 20 minutes, I call:

"Shannon, Shannon—Sacchi 252—how do you read on one twenty-four seven?"

"Good evening, Sacchi 252, Shannon reads you five by five; go ahead."

"Good evening to you. 252 is five three North and thirteen West at flight level nine zero. Estimating ten West at eighteen forty and Shannon at eighteen fifty-five."

"252, I have you as usual right where I expected you on my radar at one hundred and thirty-five miles on the two nine five degree radial. Shannon weather on the hour is two four zero at one five knots, more than ten kilometers, clouds one octare at twenty-five hundred, four octares at eight thousand, QNH one zero one three millibars, transition level five five. You are number one for approach to runway two four. How copy?"

"252 copied OK. It is a beautiful evening for a change."

"It is indeed, and the first one we've had for several days."

In a few more minutes I will request descent; I prefer to start fairly far out keeping the same power by retarding the throttle and increasing the mixture gradually as I get down into heavier air. With a small descent rate the speed will build up somewhat. This prevents the engine from cooling too fast, is easier on my ears, and saves a bit of time; as long as the air is smooth and the speed does not get too high, it is very satisfactory to me.

"Shannon, 252 requesting descent."

"252, you are cleared to transition level of five five, report reaching."

"Thank you—252 is leaving flight level nine zero."

With a rate of descent of 300 feet per minute it takes 10 minutes to reach the transition level; I am now only about 45 miles out.

"Shannon, 252 at five five and requesting further descent."

"252, we have you forty miles out; you are cleared to four thousand feet on the QNH one zero one three millibars."

(In Europe they use QNH and millibars rather than our "altimeter setting" and inches.)

"252 leaving five five for four thousand on one zero one three."

Shannon is a sea-level airport on a bend of the Shannon River about 25 miles in from the coast. This evening the weather is so clear that I can see the airport as I cross the coastline, so I call:

"Shannon—252 at four thousand crossing the coast with the airport in sight. Request visual approach."

"252, you are cleared visual to runway two four; contact tower on one one eight decimal three. Good evening."

"Good evening and thank you."

"Shannon tower, Sacchi 252 is eighteen DME West for landing."

"Good evening, Sacchi 252—this is Shannon tower; you are cleared number one for approach to runway two four, report turning final."

"252 will do. Would you advise Shell that I shall need fuel on arrival, please?"

"Will do."

"Thanks much."

Before I turn final, the tower tells me I am in sight and cleared to land. After landing he clears me to the light aircraft park, which is an area about ¼ mile from the buildings. This parking area is one of my reasons for fueling on arrival, no matter the time of night. Frequently it is raining, and the Shell people are very kind and will give me a ride to the terminal in their van. Thus I avoid the long walk with a suitcase which seems to grow heavier with each step and also stay out of the rain and wind. The other reason is that it saves quite a lot of time in the morning when there is much else to do before departure.

It's been a good trip and fairly fast with a + 25 knots on the wind for a groundspeed of 190 knots and a time of exactly 9 hours from Gander.

2 The Pilot

Any pilot who even thinks about flying a general aviation airplane across an ocean must have an adventurous streak in his/her makeup. This is a good beginning, but since ocean flying is quite different from the type of flying we do in the United States, more is required than the desire.

EXPERIENCE

The ocean-flying pilot should have had several hundred hours of cross-country experience, preferably done by pilotage and without radio, to gain confidence in meeting unexpected problems and solving them. We also need not only an instrument rating but plenty of experience on actual instruments in the clouds. It is fairly unusual to traverse the whole North Atlantic Ocean without encountering some instrument weather, and that is not the time or place to do your practicing. You will have enough other things on your mind to want the actual flying to be automatic. This includes the ability to interpret ADF bearings coming from any angle and to track to the station with any kind of wind.

The necessity of being able to track an ADF bearing with a crosswind was illustrated for me again last summer—also the desirability of being briefed by an experienced pilot before undertaking your first ocean flight.

I was delivering a Bonanza to Germany and, because of the wind, elected to go from Gander to Reykjavik, Iceland, rather than to Shannon. Air Traffic Control suggested that I listen for, and communicate with, a Twin Comanche who had departed for Iceland 2 hours before me. The straight-line distance is 1400 nautical miles; by going 20 nautical miles further you can cross the tip of Greenland; and with the fairly powerful beacon at Prince Christian you have a definitely known position at the halfway point. This seems to me worthwhile; also on that day the weather on this route was better than it was further south. I assumed that the Twin Comanche would use Prince Christian too, as the Controller had said that he was making his first flight. I was not able to hear or contact him but could hear various airliners relaying his position reports, which didn't sound like my track. Finally, somewhere between Greenland and Iceland, I heard him say that he was picking up ice. This astonished me, for as far as I could see in any direction the sky was clear; way down on the southern horizon there were some heavy clouds.

The wind was fairly strong from the Northwest, so I had a 10° drift angle applied to my heading in order to track in on the Reykjavik broadcast station. I asked a passing airliner to find out if the Twin Comanche pilot knew about this very strong station, and he said that he was using it. Somewhat later I had gained enough time on him to be able to hear his communication with Reykjavik and heard him say that he was at "Uniform," which is a reporting point 120 nautical miles West of Keflavik on my track. His estimated time for

Keflavik came and went, and to Iceland's questions, he said he was losing speed because of icing. This seemed rather peculiar because there were still no clouds within 100 miles of my track.

Finally he called that he was on the 210° radial of the Keflavik VOR and 100 miles out. This meant that he had never been within 150 miles of where he thought he was; luckily he had gotten close enough to pick up the VOR and ride it in.

I had dinner with him and his wife later and discovered that he really did not understand how to use an ADF, and had therefore been blown far off his track. Also, he had decided not to go to Prince Christian to save the extra 20 miles! Had there not been a VOR at Keflavik, as would have been the case with some other landfalls, he could easily have run out of fuel as the wind took him far South of Iceland. We will discuss the method of tracking to a station on the ADF with a crosswind in Chapter 9, Navigation.

PATIENCE AND MENTAL ATTITUDE

Once we leave the United States, everything and everybody is to some extent different from what we are used to. This is not to say that our way is necessarily better; sometimes it is not, even though we may think it is. The old saying "when in Rome, do as the Romans do" is very good advice. People in other countries, even Canada, have their own ways of doing things; you will have a much pleasanter time if you are patient and try to cooperate with them. One can't change them anyway; by accepting their methods one can make friends instead of enemies. In every country, most of the people we meet will be friendly and helpful if we are friendly. After all, our own government employees can be rather hard to get along with, too.

I did come across a Met Officer in Auckland, New Zealand, who was the exception. Everybody on the airport had been fantastically kind and helpful. After the airplane and I had been sprayed (and almost suffocated), I went into the Terminal with the Customs man, who answered my request about hotel accommodations by telephoning the one near the airport and making a reservation for me. Back on the ramp, I was standing on the wing with my tools removing the HF antenna, which had broken between Pago Pago and Tonga, so I could connect the HF to the Loran antenna, when along came a van of the local airline. The mechanic driving it asked my problem, and when I told him, he came back shortly with the airline's radio mechanic, who finished the job for me and refused any payment. That done, it was necessary to taxi down to the other end of the ramp for fueling and parking. This proved to be directly in front of the firehouse, so while I waited for the fuel truck, the firemen invited me in for a cup of coffee and conversation. Later, after the fueling was finished, they took me back to the Terminal to the hotel courtesy car (for which they had telephoned) in the fire engine, so I opened all the tourists' eyes by arriving in style. After all this hospitality I decided that New Zealanders were the nicest people in the world, and I loved them all.

It had been raining when I arrived late in the afternoon, and the sky was still threatening when it got dark, so I wondered what the weather had in store for the next day. I called the weather office from the hotel.

"Good evening, this is Louise Sacchi. I have just flown in from Pago Pago in a small airplane and am planning to go on to Melbourne, Australia, tomorrow morning. I am not asking for a forecast, but could you give me a preview of the weather along that route, and put me down for a folder at 7 A.M. local?"

Never did I expect such a reply.

"This is not your big United States. We are a small country so how should I know what the weather will be tomorrow?"

Either he had gotten out of bed on the wrong side, or some other person with an American accent had annoyed him, as this was just a rather rude non sequitur. Never before had I been refused a preview of the weather for the next day.

It is true that outside the United States you cannot call a Weather Office and expect an immediate forecast. It must be requested the evening before, which was what I was doing here, with the folder requested for a certain time in the morning; telephone briefings are rare, so be prepared. In many countries you must show the weather folder to the Information Officer before your flight plan will be accepted and approved.

Your mind must also adjust itself to the fact that for long stretches over water you will have no landmarks to tell if you are off course, so don't become impatient. This means that the wind triangles for *True* Heading, and the correct application of Variation and Deviation to find the Compass Heading which is to be flown, are really important. They must not be treated lightly. When you have determined the correct heading, you must train yourself to fly it as accurately as possible. Don't forget what we all once learned; that an angle of 1° is equal to 1 mile in every 60 miles. If the heading is wrong by 5°, at the end of 240 miles we will be off course by 20 miles.

Even on the shortest overwater legs, there still may be 200 nautical miles where remaining on track depends entirely on holding a predetermined heading until the next radio beacon can be received with accuracy. So dig out your old computer, dust it off, and practice with it. It will not be as difficult as you think, and it is a worthwhile exercise. Think of the good feeling you will have when you arrive at your destination on course and more or less on time.

The mental attitude of any copilot must also be given consideration. The left seat occupant has all the fun and excitement; the person in the right seat, unless he/she knows what is going on and can share in the planning, can get not only bored but a bit frightened by all that water, whether he/she is a pilot or a nonpilot.

On my ninety-ninth trip, I invited a friend to go along because I had time to do some sightseeing in Europe and she is good company. She is also a good pilot in her own right. To me, this was a fairly normal, uneventful trip.

A letter to her daughter tells what she thought of it (I will not tell how I came into possession of the letter).

Louise came over for a visit and said she had a new Bonanza for Switzerland and why didn't I go along. Well, sir, it all happened so fast that before I had time to give the proposition serious thought, I was on my way.

We left Philadelphia on Wednesday. We hadn't even gotten to the runway for takeoff when the one radio started fading out. So back to the radio shop. They took it apart and tested everything, and found some little pieces of scrap metal that had been rolling around inside and presumably shorted out something.

It took 5½ hours to Gander on a straight line over Boston, Nova Scotia, etc. That Newfoundland looks to be about as close to nowhere as you could get—like the surface of the moon. We spent the night there, and next day checked weather for hours—there's a lot of weather along such a distance. All tanks were filled, two 80-gallon tanks in the back seat, and the usual 80 gallons in the wings. The plane's seats and rugs and our baggage and a life raft were back of that, so when I stepped on the wing to put our water jug in, the poor thing sank down on its tail. It looked like a tired little bird. (The tail came up again when we were in our seats.)

We staggered off at about 3 P.M. local time on an instrument flight plan direct to Neuchâtel, Switzerland. Planned to arrive at 8:30 A.M. their time the next morning. Within 15 minutes we were crossing the coast eastbound and saw icebergs floating around (this in July, mind you!). In about 4 hours we were over Ocean Station Charlie. He asked, "What kind of a plane is a BE-36?"

Louise said, "It's a large Bonanza."

"How many engines?" says he.

"One," said Louise.

"There are a lot of idiots in the world," said he, at which point I picked up the mike and said, "You can say that again."

There was a pause before he said," My God, have you got a *woman* on board?"

"Two," said Louise.

It must have made his day.

We played two-handed bridge for hours, keeping score on the panel. When the sun set and there we were in the middle of the Atlantic Ocean in the middle of the night, and me not liking either night flying or overwater flying, if I'd had any beads, I would have counted them.

It was mostly a smooth flight with one short period of real turbulence some time during the night. The Artificial Horizon quit soon after Gander, the HF radio kept blowing fuses, and the Low Voltage Warning Light kept flashing on—as if I needed anything to keep me awake! But the engine ground soothingly on.

Ocean Station Juliet was about two-thirds of the way across and the horizon began to show a faint light. When we had used the last spare fuse for the HF radio and it blew again, Louise asked "Juliet" to give Shannon our position, but in a little while on emergency frequency comes a Cubana Airline calling us to say that Shannon wanted to know where the hell are we.

Eleven and a half hours out we crossed over Land's End, England; in thirteen hours we were over Chartres and the continent but it was solid clouds. We got as far as Dijon and when we checked the weather at Geneva again, it was so crumby that we had to turn back and go into Paris (IFR of course). They have *very* scary approaches there. We sat on the ground there for a few hours and then pressed on when the worst part had gone. Descended through the clouds at Geneva and then under the clouds up the valley to Neuchâtel.

PHYSICAL CONSIDERATIONS

Once your mind is adjusted to the different environment which will be encountered, it is equally important to plan for your body's needs. It is extremely foolish to fast on such a flight; one's brain needs food and fluid to function at its best in unaccustomed circumstances.

I have found that a supply of cheese to eat and water to drink is the minimum satisfactory nourishment for either hot or cold weather. Naturally, this can be varied to suit one's individual tastes, depending on the season; some foods remain edible only in fairly cold weather. Sweet things are best avoided because the lift you get from them dissipates quickly and they tend to increase thirst. And of course, eating gives you something to do while you are wondering whether you are still on course and making good your estimated groundspeed.

Some sort of container (or other method) for emptying the bladder is essential because a full bladder will get so painful that it interferes with the thinking process. Men have the advantage here, but a bit of ingenuity will provide the same relief for a woman. Naturally it will be more complicated to arrange if there are mixed sexes in a small airplane.

Be a bit careful about what you eat and drink at overnight and lunch stops, remembering there is not an airport under you every 50 miles or so in case of need for other than bladder problems. I always carry a small bottle of apple cider vinegar of which I put a teaspoon or so in any glass of water. It is refreshing, improves the taste of some otherwise bad tasting water, and, more important, helps prevent any food poisoning and consequent diarrhea, even in places like Mexico, South America, Africa, and Asia. Very cheap health insurance. In temperate climates the food is normally perfectly safe, and the local dishes can be quite delicious and different.

A pair of good sunglasses is practically a must, prescription ones if you normally wear glasses either for distance or for reading. Flying at 9000 feet, one is usually on top of the clouds (and there are always clouds over some part of the ocean), and the sun on the clouds or on the icecap of Greenland can be quite blinding.

NOTE: Perhaps most important of all, do not allow yourself to be tempted into flying at higher than 10,000 feet without *oxygen*. If your airplane has a turbocharged engine, *be sure you have sufficient oxygen* for the number of hours you will be higher than that. No matter how young and healthy you think you are, prolonged flight at high altitude without oxygen is *extremely dangerous*.

I recently lost a friend who always said, "Altitude doesn't

bother me, I am healthy and I don't smoke" whenever I tried to argue with him about flying high just because his engine was turbocharged. He was a very experienced pilot with a good bit of ocean experience as well, but anoxia finally caught up with him.

We need the increased oxygen in low-level air just as an engine does; the oxygen bottle is to us as the turbocharger is to the engine.

3 The Airplane

It makes no real difference whether your airplane has one or two engines or a high or low wing; this is a matter of choice with each pilot. One type is as safe as another, assuming they are in equally good condition. Between one engine and two each has advantages and disadvantages.

If the engine of a single-engine airplane quits, you are obviously going to ditch in a few minutes; how long depends on your altitude and glide ratio at the gross weight when the engine fails.

If one engine of a twin-engine airplane fails *after* you have burned enough fuel to be down to or below normal gross weight, your chances are better of making it safely to an airport. These chances are not so good while the airplane is still over normal gross weight. However, we have all discovered (although we may not have realized what it was) that there is a cushion of air which extends up from the ground or water about the distance of one-half the span of our wing. Remember the times when we were trying to make a landing and the airplane kept on floating? Certainly it would not be easy to remain in this cushion of compressed air, but if a pilot was precise enough in his flying, it would be possible and would assist the other engine in keeping the airplane in the air until reaching land again.

I once heard over the Pacific Ocean the pilot of a light twin call Mayday because he had lost one engine and the other one was overheating, so he was about to shut it down and ditch. He was about 500 miles offshore. Several voices chimed in to tell him that before shutting down the other engine and ditching he should try getting down to about 50 feet over the sea into this cushion of air. By opening the cowl flaps on the operating engine maybe he could make it back to land or at least stay in the air until Air-Sea Rescue found him. It happened that an alert MATS airplane spotted him and radioed his position to the Rescue airplane. With everybody in the area encouraging him, his panic subsided and he managed to fly close to the water. Soon the Rescue airplane was over him and giving him advice about headings and engine operation. The weather was perfect and not hot enough to destroy any of his airplane's performance; the wind was on his tail going back, and while it was fairly light, still it was some help. Everything was in his favor, and with the Rescue airplane over him all the way, he managed to make it back to California. Not all twin-engine pilots have been so lucky, but that pilot's experience proves it is possible.

If some system fails (say the alternator or vacuum/pressure pump, etc.) on a single-engine airplane, you will lose the instruments or electrical equipment dependent on that system.

In most twin-engine airplanes, if the system fails on one engine, there is the same system on the other engine to keep you in business until the next intended landing. So this is another point in favor of the twin-engine plane.

However let's look at the other side of the argument of twin- versus single-engine airplanes.

For some mysterious reason the engine which is trouble-free when it is installed in the nose of a single-engine airplane tends to have problems of one kind or another when installed in the wing of a twin-engine airplane. Engine failures cause more fatal accidents in twins than in singles because the pilot has become complacent and not acquired or kept up proficiency in flying with one engine out with its attendant aerodynamic unbalances.

If the individual legs of your proposed trip involve really long distances between possible fuel stops, so that extra fuel in the cabin is a must, the single-engine airplane has an advantage over the twin-engine one. Neither the cabin size nor the Useful Load of an average light twin-engine airplane will be twice that of a comparable single-engine airplane, but you will have two engines to feed rather than one; therefore the latter will have a definite edge in range/endurance. Table 3-1 shows a typical example of two airplanes using the same engine and standard 10 percent over gross weight for ferry. If the single-engine plane cruises at 160 knots and the twin at 175 knots (this is an average difference at any given power), we have an added range for the

TABLE 3-1

	Single	Twin
Normal Gross Weight	3400 lb	5200 lb
Empty Weight	−2100 lb	−3200 lb
Useful Load	1300 lb	2000 lb
10% Normal Gross	+ 340 lb	+ 520 lb
Useful Load in Ferry Use	1640 lb	2520 lb
Pilot, Baggage, Emergency equipment, HF radio, and Loran	− 255 lb	− 255 lb
	1385 lb	2265 lb
Tanks, mounting, plumbing	− 110 lb	− 150 lb
Available fuel weight	1275 lb	2115 lb
Fuel in Wings	(80 gal) − 480 lb	(160 gal) − 960 lb
Extra fuel	795 lb	1155 lb
Divided by 6 lb/gal	132 gal	192 gal
Each engine burns 12 gal/h	11:00 h	8:00 h

single of 1760 nautical miles and for the twin of 1400 nautical miles.

As you can see, the difference in speed between the two types of airplanes is not enough to compensate for the loss of air time of the twin. Since engines are more reliable these days than wind and weather forecasts, the added range of the single is to me a significant advantage.

The airplane you choose should have fuel in the wings for 5 to 6 hours at 65 percent cruise power and a respectable airspeed. I could not recommend an airplane which cruises at less than 130 knots because it will make even a fairly short ocean leg seem quite long and tiring. Also, it exposes one for a longer period of time to possible unforecast adverse winds.

There must be sufficient Useful Load to carry full fuel, the person or persons who are planning to go, and their luggage and necessary emergency equipment and still be able to take extra fuel in the cabin without exceeding the normal ferry limit of 110 percent gross weight. This eliminates any airplane which is not a true four-placer.

If the still-air range is less than 900 nautical miles, it is foolish to go without extra fuel. Alternate airports are far, far away, where there are any at all. You are "betting your bottom dollar" on the accuracy of the forecast wind and weather. To accommodate all this weight, the center of gravity envelope needs to be fairly wide; otherwise, you will end up trying to put everything and everybody in the same spot to stay within center of gravity limits. It goes without saying that luggage must be held to a minimum; if you have a lot, send it ahead on an airline and pick it up when you arrive.

The least expensive, simplest, and most error-proof tanking can be done in the low-wing single-engine airplane, as it does not need electric fuel pumps for the cabin tanks (Figure 3-1). They can feed the engine by gravity through a simple ON-OFF valve. High-wing and twin-engine airplanes almost always need electric fuel pumps for the cabin tanks to feed properly. One can use either drums or specially built steel tanks, the size being determined by cabin space, the chosen route, and the desired range.

Any of the cabin tank installations will require an FAA ferry permit until crossing the border of the United States, as the airplane is not in its normal, approved configuration. A ferry permit allows only crew members on the flight—no passengers—so this is another good reason for getting the prospective right seat occupant involved in the mechanics of the flight, and, unless you have quite a large airplane, for restricting the occupants to two.

If you are planning to use any of the bigger, corporate-type twins, you will be in clover, as they usually have both

FIGURE 3-1

Right-hand tank with HF radio on top. Left-hand tank behind the pilot's seat leaves plenty of legroom for tall people. The Loran will sit on the step of the right-hand tank after the pilot is ensconced in his seat.

the range and speed as well as the Useful Load to make the trip with passengers and without difficulty. If the airplane is either a turbo-prop or pure jet and normally cruises above 27,000 feet, there will be different rules in the navigation department from those for flights in the lower levels of the atmosphere.

Speaking of the second crew member reminds me of an abortive attempt to convert an airline pilot to a ferry pilot which I tried a few years ago. He is a friend of long standing, from the "good old days" before World War II when flying was more relaxed and fewer pilots were competing for space in the sky. We enjoyed many Sunday afternoons playing in my J-3 Cub, and I learned a lot about flying from him. Then he went into the Navy and to an airline; over the next 30 years he rose to the top, Senior Captain on overseas runs in 707 and 747 types. Small airplanes were no longer part of his life, but in due course came retirement and he was very sad. Ocean flying was what he really wanted, so I suggested he might like to do some ferrying and invited him to try it with me in a Cessna 206 I was taking to Germany; this idea appealed to him.

Because he had once taught me, and because of his exalted position as a Senior Captain, I assumed that a simple airplane could pose no problems for him. We left Boston with him in the right seat; once airborne and on course, I turned over the controls to him, only mentioning the desired heading to Yarmouth, Nova Scotia. In a very few minutes we were aiming at Portugal rather than Yarmouth. I finally said something about the instruments being hard to read from the right seat, and perhaps a correction to the heading would be in order. He agreed and for a few minutes we were going toward Yarmouth, but pretty quickly Baffin Land drew us. I had noticed but hesitated to mention that his feet were firmly planted on the floor, and the wheel was really getting a workout. Eventually I had to say, "These little airplanes are not as stable as a 747; they really are easier to fly with your feet on the rudder pedals."

He tried, he really did, but it was foreign to everything he had been doing for many years in the big ones. So we wove our way to Gander, more or less at 9000 feet, and landed.

His astonishment was great when we did not step out of the airplane and drive off to the hotel but instead stayed for the fueling and checked the oil, took the airplane to its parking place, installed the chocks and control lock, went to Customs, signed in the airport log, went to the Weather Bureau to look at the ocean weather picture, and only then went to the hotel.

Very early next morning, without breakfast, we went to the Weather Bureau and received a thorough ocean briefing. We were given a weather folder which we took down to the cafeteria to figure the flight plan with our after-breakfast coffee. A 150-knot flight plan is puzzling to a 450-knot pilot; for one thing it has too many reporting points. Tramp to the other end of the building to the Air Traffic Control office to file the flight plan, back down to the airport office to pay the fees (Gander has a "garbage" fee, too), make the last "pit stop," then find the attendant to open the door to the ramp, and out to the airplane for a thorough preflight check (after all, the next airport is 1700 nautical miles away!); and then we were ready to embark.

It would be an 11-hour flight to Shannon, which is long by airline standards. The left seat is less tiring to fly in, as the instruments can be read without straining your neck, so that's where he sat. This time I did remind him to use his feet on the rudder pedals, and that, since we lacked the dual INS he was accustomed to, heading and ADF were our only means of finding Shannon, Ireland, 11 hours away. We were partly on top and partly in clouds, so by the time we got to Ocean Station Charlie, after 4 hours, my poor friend was really exhausted. That kind of instrument flying is really hard work, as we all know; so he asked me to fly and he went to sleep for an hour before he took over again.

Eventually we arrived at Shannon and the same routine: park the airplane, fuel it, walk a half mile to the terminal, clear Customs, check in with the Airport Duty Office, go to the Weather Bureau, and then walk over to the hotel.

In the morning again pretty much as at Gander, breakfast, flight plan, pay airport fees, preflight airplane, then embark. When we arrived in Germany, his comment was, "I had no idea there was so much to do; I don't see how ferry pilots manage it all."

It really is too much of a transition for the average Senior Airline Captain, who is used to a crew and ground dispatcher to do most of the work, an autopilot to do most of the flying, and Inertial Navigation Systems to do the navigating, to come down to a not very stable single-engine airplane with minimal equipment. Had his first shot at ferrying been in a well-equipped twin, I might not have lost one who could have been a good and enthusiastic ferry pilot. He was, and still is, only happy with wings under him.

INSTRUMENTS AND AVIONICS

The instruments and avionics needed for a well-equipped instrument airplane in the United States are equally necessary for flying across the ocean and in any foreign country.

One of the most important items, because it may well be your only aid to navigation, is a really good ADF which can reach out 150 to 200 nautical miles; additionally it must have a Beat Frequency Oscillator (BFO). Radio emissions in other countries are often different from ours, and only the BFO makes it possible to read their identification.

The Canadian Department of Transport requires that a single- but not a twin-engine airplane departing on overwater flight have two direction-finding radios of which at least one must have BFO. The second ADF does give a nice sense of security in that, hopefully, both will not fail at the same time. However, a portable range receiver with its loop antenna is not only acceptable but preferred by some of the inspectors because of its separate power supply. Since departures from North America across the Atlantic normally leave from a Canadian airport and their Search and Rescue area extends halfway to Europe, they do have the final word on our equipment.

You also need at least one VHF transceiver with 360 or 720 channels; fewer channels are useless for communications in other countries. One or two VORs with localizer capability and a transponder with altitude-reporting capability are a must.

As it is in the United States, additional items such as a glide-slope, DME, RMI, autopilot, etc., are very nice and certainly make things easier. You can get along without them, but they are the frosting on the cake.

ADDITIONAL EQUIPMENT

For the ocean flight you will also need a High Frequency (HF) transceiver for position reporting and other communications with ground stations. This radio operates in the 2000- to 13,000-kilohertz band, and most of them come with ten channels. It enables one to communicate over distances of up to 1500 nautical miles or more.

Plan ahead so that perhaps you can rent one, as they are very expensive to buy these days. The HF radio operates either on a fixed antenna, if it has a load unit, or more cheaply on a variable-length trailing antenna, which is wound in and out from a reel, either by hand or by electric motor.

The hand-operated reel has an added advantage beside cost; there will be a hole in the floor for the antenna mast, and this hole can be used with a relief tube, thus eliminating the bottle which must be emptied on arrival.

The frequency in use determines the length of the trailing wire; the lower the frequency the longer the wire. In the daytime the most used frequencies are in the 8800- to 8900-kilohertz range, which takes approximately 18 to 20 feet. In the early morning or late evening 5600 kilohertz works better and requires 36 to 40 feet of wire. The really low frequencies, 2800 and 2900 kilohertz, are used at night and will give your arm a good workout as they need 85 to 90 feet of antenna. Letting it out is easy enough, but bringing it in is a real task, and the faster the airplane the harder the reeling in.

A flashlight is a really useful item of equipment, even if you are not planning any night flights. There are always the times you get caught out after dark and/or drop something vital in a dark place. Even domestically, it is handy for finding birds' nests or dead things in the wheel wells and tail cones.

I always carry a few basic tools: regular and Phillips screwdrivers in a couple of sizes, pliers, cutters, and a few common size wrenches. Probably they will not be needed, but one can feel very silly if they are needed and not on board. Also some tape, both masking and electric, will come in handy. It is surprising how many uses there are for tape; one use I make of it is for sticking charts or weather folders on the windshield and side windows to keep the sun off me in tropical areas or in the summer on the North Atlantic.

More than once I have needed the tools myself or have come across another pilot who needed them and so was able to be of help. At many large airports either there is nobody who has tools, or the person who might have some is clear at the other end of the airport.

A set of chocks as well as the control locks and pitot cover are good things to have; almost never does one find chocks on any airport and of course no tiedowns either. So far I've never lost an airplane to the wind, but I have spent some uneasy nights listening to it blow, especially in winter.

And *again* I remind you, if you think there is the slightest possibility that you will want to fly above 10,000 feet, *be sure* that you have adequate *oxygen* with you, even if it means leaving something else behind. Remember, "the life you save may be your own."

PREPARATION OF THE AIRPLANE
BEFORE DEPARTURE

Looking through my notebooks for helpful suggestions, I came across a flight which reminded me that a stitch in time saves nine; instrument flying is much, much easier if all instruments are working. I picked up a new airplane which had been sitting out on the line at the factory for several days awaiting payment. Everything seemed to check out all right so we (the owner was with me) departed Eastbound to get the ferry tanks installed. After stopping for fuel at Dayton we came to the overcast over the Alleghenies; rather than bounce around underneath I elected to go on top at 9000 feet. We sat up there for over 1 hour, and I was quietly congratulating myself on doing such a splendid job of holding altitude and airspeed—really phenomenal because the needles never moved from their appointed places.

Then it came time to descend through the clouds into Philadelphia, which had 1000 feet and 4 miles, so there were several thousand feet of cloud. What do you know? Even when I started the descent, none of the needles moved; as far as they were concerned, I was still at 9000 feet. Now what? Turning to the alternate air did not improve matters as the airspeed went to zero, the altimeter jumped up 500 feet, and the rate of climb said 200 feet per minute *up*. Modern airplanes, of course, do not have wires and struts to sing in the wind with different voices at different speeds, so all I could do was to leave things pretty much alone, since I had already trimmed it for descent, and judge my altitude by the increase in manifold pressure as we came down. I did advise Approach Control that I might be a bit sloppy in maintaining an altitude while in the clouds. Fortunately, the ceiling and visibility were better than advertised so there was no problem.

When we checked the static-system drain, we found that it had about half a cup of water in it. Of course, all the instruments had to be dried out before we went further.

Whether the airplane is new or not so new, if it has been tied down outside with or without a pitot cover, find and check the static-system drain. The airspeed, altimeter, and rate of climb all depend for information on dry air from the static system. Water can and does collect in the line, especially from a driving rain or snow. Remember those little holes in the side of the fuselage? Insects like to build nests in the pitot head, and then the airspeed goes, and I suppose there are other things I haven't even heard of which can foul up this important system.

Pitot heat is a necessity for any airplane which is used for instrument flying. It is even more important for an airplane flying across the North Atlantic at any time of year. Be very sure the pitot heat is working before leaving home base; one that is not working is worse than useless and can be dangerous because of false airspeed readings, although it usually ends up reading zero. In those latitudes if there is any visible moisture, the pitot system will ice up before there is any trace of ice on the windshield. Should this happen, one can still fly fairly safely by using the trim tab and the rate of climb to maintain level flight or to climb and descend at safe speed. The danger of overcontrolling and stalling only occurs when the pilot manhandles the elevators. With hands in lap and flying with rudder and trim tab one is quite safe.

The fuel system sometimes gets less thought given to it than it should get. Even carburetors do not take kindly to either dirt or water in their innards; injectors absolutely refuse to have any commerce with them, so be sure that your tanks, screens, lines, and all other parts of the system have nothing but clean fuel in them.

If your tires and/or brakes are near the point where you say to yourself, "I'll have to change them soon," do it now before you go. Any parts you must replace will be much more expensive overseas than they are here, if you can even find them; you might have to wait until they are shipped to you from home.

Hydraulic systems and electric motors for flaps and landing gear need to be checked to be sure that they are still efficient and if not, made so. There are, of course, very good mechanics in Iceland and Europe, but they may not have parts for your brand of airplane.

I was once very fortunate when an alternator belt on a twin-engine airplane broke between Gander and Reykjavik. It was a new airplane but the belt had been installed carelessly and was rubbing on a piece of metal. There were no aircraft belts of the right size available at Reykjavik, but David, the excellent mechanic there, managed to find one that would fit at an auto supply store in town. While I was waiting, I checked the other one very carefully. Since it was OK, I started tossing a mental coin to decide whether I would go with only one alternator if he couldn't find a belt.

In problems like this, as we said earlier, the twin-engine airplane has an advantage over the single-engine airplane. In the single I obviously could not think of going without a working alternator.

An ocean flight is not something you will decide on today for tomorrow's departure, so you will have plenty of time to pay attention to all these things and others which I may have forgotten. Just be sure that everything is shipshape before embarking on this delightful adventure so you can enjoy it to the full.

4 The Engine or Engines

E ngines in the United States—and indeed in all the free world—come principally from two manufacturers, Continental and Lycoming. As far as reliability is concerned, I have found no difference between them. Each has its little idiosyncrasies, but if you own your airplane or rent the same one frequently, you will have discovered and compensated for them before you prepare for your trip.

For some reason, as mentioned earlier, an engine mounted in the wing of a twin-engine airplane seems more likely to develop problems than the exact same engine mounted in the nose of a single-engine airplane. The only way I can account for this is the difference in cowling and airflow and the variation in vibration frequency between the wing and the nose. A wing-mounted engine is much more tightly cowled and is mounted at a quite different angle.

I have also noticed a difference in reliability with the same engine in different makes of airplanes and suspect this has the same cause.

This comparison of wing-mounted versus nose-mounted engines is one reason I have no hesitation in crossing an ocean with a single-engine airplane. Another reason is that the engine has no eyes; therefore it cannot see that it is over water. Since it is not afraid of "all that water," it just keeps on running for its allotted number of hours, regardless of what is under it. Also I have never heard of a Mayday because of engine failure in a single-engine airplane. They have occurred when the pilot ran out of fuel or oil, and one is as bad as the other here, but neither of those can be blamed on the engine itself.

Since the airplane you will want for such a trip must have an adequate Useful Load and a respectable speed, it will need an engine of at least 180 horsepower, preferably more. There is only one engine I am aware of in this class which does not have fuel injection, so my remarks will be addressed primarily to the fuel-injected engine.

AGE AND CONDITION

The age of an engine is not as important as its condition. The manufacturers have given their engines a time between overhauls (TBO) life of 1200 to about 2000 hours. This, of course, does not mean that the engine will collapse completely at that point; rather it means that the wear will be such that the engine is no longer as efficient; and some parts may start breaking down. However, when we are planning to set forth across an ocean, with no place to "pull off the road" in case of trouble, it makes more sense to use an engine which is not beyond its half-life.

On the other hand, I will not set forth with a brand new or newly overhauled engine until it has some time on it. Like any mechanical gadget, it can break down in either minor or major ways in the first few hours. So fly it for at least 25 hours or so at high power to be sure that all systems are in good working order.

FUEL CONSUMPTION, POWER, AND SPEED

Our modern, efficient engines have a specific fuel consumption of approximately $1/2$ pound of fuel per horsepower-hour for good cooling. Aviation fuel weighs 6 pounds per gallon (jet fuel is approximately 7 pounds per gallon). These figures enable one to determine the length of time one can stay aloft at any given horsepower.

However, for long distance, or ocean flying, the speed at which we fly is important; this depends on the type of wing, the weight of the airplane, and the angle at which the wing pushes through the air. If you must fly at a high angle of attack to stay up, the loss of speed from the inefficient angle of the wing will more than offset the longer fuel endurance. There is a power setting below which you will defeat your prime purpose, which is to make the long flight in as short a time as possible and with as large a fuel reserve as possible.

Most airplane-engine combinations are engineered to give the most efficient speed/fuel-consumption ratio at between 55 and 65 percent power. During World War II, when the principles of really long-distance flying were just being developed, the engineers' figures seemed to indicate that 45 percent power would work the best. These were engineering figures on paper; the pilots who had to fly their heavily laden airplanes across the ocean to England finally revolted at wallowing through the air at such a low speed with its sloppy control response. Eventually they discovered by trying that they arrived with more fuel reserve and of course in a shorter time by increasing the power enough so that the wing could really fly at an efficient angle. A 45 percent power setting may be good for endurance, if one wishes to set an endurance record, but not for reasonable time enroute.

When I first started flying across oceans, I had read all the books and studied the charts and graphs of range and endurance at various power settings. I kept careful records for myself, the condensed results of which are shown in Table 4-1. The same results were obtained with all the different engine-airplane combinations I delivered; these pretty well ran the gamut of what is available in general aviation airplanes of both one and two engines. As you will see from the table, the best compromise on speed versus fuel consumption is at 58 percent power; below that the speed drops so fast that the time enroute and fuel consumption for the trip increase unacceptably.

The question of a maximum climb versus a cruise climb to altitude is another which seems to have proponents on both sides. I have found such minor differences in overall fuel consumption from one to the other that I prefer a modified cruise climb at a reasonable airspeed for engine cooling and to reach my cruising altitude over some definite point to start checking enroute groundspeed.

For descent, there is no question in my mind that the most efficient way is to keep my cruise power by retarding the throttle to keep the power constant as I descend at a rate of about 300 feet per minute. This allows the airspeed to build up somewhat and keeps the engine warm. It also shortens the time a bit and is easier on my ears. Of course, there are times when the Controller will not allow this gradual descent; then if you cannot cancel your IFR and proceed visually, you must try to keep the engine warm on descent by other means, such as slowing up enough to lower the gear to enable you to lose altitude with a fair amount of power. Rapid and/or prolonged cooling does the engine no good, particularly if you then require increased power from it because of a balked landing or any other such problem.

In planning an ocean flight, fuel reserve is one of the first considerations; the longer the ocean leg the greater reserve we will want because of the possibility of inaccurate wind forecasts.

When considering your rate of fuel consumption at any given power setting, consider the following. Many power

TABLE 4-1

TAS	GS	760		1700		2100	
		Time, h	Gal	Time, h	Gal	Time, h	Gal
0 Wind Condition, Neither Help nor Hindrance							
Single-Engine, 285 hp:							
63% = 13.5 gal/h = 168 kn		4:30	61	10:10	137	12:30	169
58% = 12.2 gal/h = 160 kn		4:45	58	10:40	130	13:05	160
50% = 11.0 gal/h = 143 kn		5:20	59	11:55	131	14:45	162
Twin-Engine, 570 hp:							
63% = 27.0 gal/h = 183 kn		4:10	111	9:20	252	11:25	307
58% = 24.5 gal/h = 173 kn		4:25	107	9:50	240	12:05	298
50% = 22.0 gal/h = 155 kn		4:55	108	11:00	242	13:35	300
−20 Wind Condition, 20-kn Headwind							
Single-Engine, 285 hp:							
63% = 13.5 gal/h = 168 kn	(148 kn)	5:05	69	11:30	155	14:10	192
58% = 12.2 gal/h = 160 kn	(140 kn)	5:25	66	12:05	147	15:00	183
50% = 11.0 gal/h = 143 kn	(123 kn)	6:10	68	13:50	152	17:05	188
Twin-Engine, 570 hp:							
63% = 27.0 gal/h = 183 kn	(163 kn)	4:40	125	10:25	280	12:50	345
58% = 24.5 gal/h = 173 kn	(153 kn)	4:55	120	11:05	272	13:40	335
50% = 22.0 gal/h = 155 kn	(135 kn)	5:35	123	12:40	279	15:35	342

Trip length, nmi

computers and power charts—perhaps all of them—give flow figures for peak power and peak temperatures. Both Continental and Lycoming advise that with a high-compression engine the cooling should be done with fuel; in other words the mixture should be slightly richer than the power computer indicates. Depending on the engine, this will take an additional $1/2$ to 1 gallon per hour. If you are using an exhaust gas temperature (EGT) gage, it will be 50 to 75° on the rich side of peak temperature. Unfortunately, I know a few pilots who slavishly set their fuel flow by the computer and completely disregard the roughness of the poor, protesting engine. This will shorten engine life.

CARE AND FEEDING OF ENGINES

It seems to me that one of the most important things a person can do to be kind to his/her engine and ensure its happiness and long, trouble-free life is to run it at *full power* for at least the first 25 to 30 hours. By full power I mean push the throttle to the firewall on takeoff and *leave* it there until ready for descent; when just airborne pull the prop back 25 rpm from the red line and *leave* it there. In using this procedure check the owner's manual for limits on low altitude and/or high ambient temperatures.

With the throttle full forward, the engine is in a maximum rich position; this ensures proper engine cooling in a steep climb at low airspeed. Naturally, leaning should be done as climb speed increases after the first few hundred feet of altitude are gained, to prevent an over-rich mixture which will cool the cylinders too much and tend to foul the plugs. With the prop at high rpm, the pistons go up and down more times per minute, giving the piston rings a better chance of seating against the cylinder walls. When the rings are seated, they prevent the oil from getting into the combustion chamber of the cylinder; the spark plugs, particularly the bottom ones, do not get oil-soaked, and the engine can then put out its rated power, which is based on burning gasoline and not oil.

This same technique can be applied to older engines which are burning oil. I once had to deliver a used Baron with Continental IO-470 engines which had 400 hours on them. When I got the airplane, each engine was burning 1 quart of oil per hour; the arithmetic of a 10-quart capacity and a 9-hour flight left something to be desired. I changed the oil and flew the airplane locally at full power and high rpm at 7000 feet for 4 hours. At the end of that time, each engine needed 1½ quarts. Things were looking up, and I departed for Gander at full power, which was another 4-hour flight. At Gander each engine needed only 1 quart, so the 1700 plus nautical miles to Shannon was quite feasible. My satisfaction was great when on arrival at Shannon, after 8 hours and 30 minutes, I found that only about a pint could have been squeezed in each engine.

This indicates that if we buy a used airplane which seems to have had good care but still is burning oil, it is worthwhile to suspect that the former owner "babied" his engine and that some hard running will cure it. Piston rings will never seat at low power. Cylinders which have been chromed on overhaul have a much harder surface than standard and will require more hours of full-power operation to seat their rings.

As long as this flying is done at or above 1500 feet and with adequate fuel flow for cooling, it is not possible to hurt the engine.

Some or all of this full-power flying should be done above 5000 feet to check the health of the ignition system. The reason for this is that if you have defective magnetos, ignition harness, or spark plugs, reduced air density will allow the spark to jump from its normal pathway to the nearest point and the engine will miss. If the engine runs smoothly at low altitudes but gets progressively rougher (usually on one magneto) as the altitude increases above 5000 feet, it is almost surely an ignition problem.

Another thing which bothers me when I see it—and I see it often—is a pilot who either does not drain the fuel sumps and strainers before flight or drains the fuel onto the ground.

Long ago I discovered the hard way that fuel-injected engines (most modern engines are fuel-injected) do not take kindly to dirt in their fuel. In fact they complain loudly and bitterly about it. If one drains the fuel onto the ground, there is no way to tell whether there is dirt or water in it. Particularly in new airplanes this has caused many people a lot of grief and some forced landings.

Primarily, this is because the symptoms can lead a mechanic to suspect an ignition problem rather than a fuel problem; it depends on how the pilot describes the problem and what questions the mechanic asks. I know more than a few owners who have spent much time and money having the ignition system pulled apart and various new parts installed time after time without any change in the problem.

When they are finally persuaded to check the fuel strainers and screens, they find dirt or, worse, fuzz, which has gone right through the system and into the injector nozzles in the individual cylinders, clogging them so the fuel cannot get through.

New fuel tanks all too frequently have fuzz from the manufacturing process embedded in the material. When the fuel sloshes around in the tank, as it does in flight, this fuzz is gradually leached out of the tank walls and is then free in the fuel. It starts on its merry way through the tank screen, into the lines, through the injector screen (which is an extremely small mesh), into the distributor, and on into the nozzles. Big dirt is bad enough, but most of it will be caught in the tank strainer; fuzz, on the other hand, is difficult to see and is small enough to go on through to the nozzles.

The clear plastic fuel drainer which is available at almost every airport is certainly cheap insurance. If you drain the fuel into it and hold it up to the light with a critical eye, you can see the teeny bits of fuzz floating around and take steps (Figure 4-1). Should you see this danger sign, it is wise to drain and flush the tanks and flush the system right on through to the nozzles.

Take the nozzles out of the cylinders and put small glass or clear plastic containers under each one; turn the boost

FIGURE 4-1

Fuel tank sumps and strainer should be checked with a clear plastic tube after each refuelling and overnight stop. If dirt, fuzz, or water is found, leave drain open until fuel runs clear. Clean fuel helps the engine to run smoothly.

pump on high with the mixture in full rich. You can tell by the variation in the amount of fuel in each container whether one or more cylinders are getting a greater or lesser flow than the others; thus you know if any of them are clogged either at the nozzle or possibly at the distributor.

The most prominent in-flight symptom of fuzz in the fuel system is an engine which is running rough at all altitudes and all power settings above idle. If increasing the fuel flow well above normal helps to keep the engine from trying to jump out of its mounts, you are fairly sure that fuel is your problem.

Before I got smart enough to take early precautions, I became quite expert at pulling out screens and nozzles on cold, windswept, and rainswept ramps. Sometimes I spent days waiting for a new set of nozzles (or a distributor) when the nozzles I had were beyond cleaning because they had developed leaks from clogging. Once I had to turn back after 2 hours over the ocean and wondered whether the engines would run long enough to make it. You can see why I feel strongly about always using the plastic drainer to check the fuel before each flight.

As important to combustion as fuel is air. Part of the fuel system check should be to ensure that the air filter on the front of the engine is clean so that the engine will get its allotted amount of air. Also be sure that the alternate air source for the engine is available in case the normal, outside air inlet becomes blocked with ice. If the engine can maintain power and the prop remain free of ice, the airplane will fly surprisingly well with a fairly good load of ice on the wings. Not that I am recommending flying in ice, but if you get caught, don't panic; you will have time to find another altitude where there is at least no more accumulation.

OIL CAPACITY, CONSUMPTION, AND COOLING

Oil consumption can sometimes be the determining factor in whether one's engine is adequate for crossing the ocean. An engine in good condition should not burn more than 1 quart in 5 to 6 hours. If it does and you cannot cure it with the methods outlined above, don't consider going. It will do you no good to have ample fuel if the engine runs out of oil, and carrying extra oil to add during flight is definitely not practicable (Figure 4-2).

Oil coolers can be a source of trouble too. Some engines mount their oil coolers on the front of the engine just behind the prop. Certainly this ensures adequate cooling, but at certain times of the year it also ensures a possibility of trouble from too much cooling. These engines normally have a special oil-cooler baffle to keep the oil from congealing in the cores; it is important to install this baffle in cold weather and just as important to remove it when the weather warms up. Without baffles the oil will start to con-

FIGURE 4-2
Check the oil before departure and at each stop to record the rate of engine usage. This should be done as nearly as possible at the same oil temperature; either when the engine is hot after shutdown, or when it is cold before startup.

geal in the cooler cores at approximately 20°F. When this happens, the circulation between cooler and crankcase is cut down, and the remaining circulating oil has more work to do; consequently it gets quite hot and the pressure falls exactly as it would if you had burned too much oil and had only a little left. Seeking a warmer altitude is the answer, and as soon as possible. The oil will start to flow again at 34°F or above. This can be a very uncomfortable situation when there are no airports handy.

One can also have a problem in warm weather if one forgets to remove the baffles. Particularly in climb when using high power at a fairly low speed, the diminished area of the cooler exposed to the air blast cannot keep up with the cooling needs of the hard-working oil, and so again the pressure falls as the temperature rises.

These cooler passages are quite small, and in older airplanes it is not only possible but probable that they will become clogged just as the oil screen and/or filter would if they were not cleaned at frequent intervals. Should you encounter odd or different oil pressure/temperature readings, it is worth investigating the cooler and its vernitherm valve.

ELECTRICAL SYSTEM

Another important part of an engine is the electrical system. While the engine itself will run happily without it once it is started (unlike a car), we will have neither lighting nor communications and navigation without it and no way of activating the flaps and landing gear if they are electric, this is the reason for the emergency landing gear hand crank.

This system includes the generator or alternator, voltage regulator and overvoltage relay, battery, ammeter and/or voltmeter, and various fuses or circuit breakers, associated wiring, and warning lights. Because any of these components can, and every so often do, break down, I always carry a volt monitor to give me early warning before any problem develops into a major one and a source of danger to the airplane and its avionic equipment.

There are several of these monitors on the market, but the one I prefer is a Lamar Volt Monitor, which is a simple two-light instrument; I plug it into the cigarette lighter because I am always in a different airplane. The friends to whom I have given one own their airplanes so have mounted it on the instrument panel in a permanent installation connected to the main bus.

The amber light shows low voltage. It not only warns of complete generator or alternator failure immediately but also tells you that the circuit is overloaded or that there is trouble in the wiring. With too low voltage radios will not get enough power to operate properly, which is detrimental to both communications and navigation. It also warns that you forgot to turn off the master switch when shutting down—and who has not forgotten occasionally and found a dead battery on the next flight?

The red light warns of overvoltage, which is more dangerous because, for one thing, the battery acid may boil over and cause damage. Additionally, too high voltage will fuse and burn all the delicate insides of your radios and autopilot, so you find yourself with the very large expense of repairing or replacing them. If you have an easily seen red light to give instantaneous warning, it is possible to turn everything off before any major damage is done, and when you do go to the radio shop you know exactly what happened. This will save the radio mechanic some time, as he knows what to look for.

So—the electrical system needs to be thoroughly checked out and put in peak condition before your trip. Even on a new airplane disagreeable things can happen to it, as I found out one night.

I was delivering a new Sundowner to Barcelona in Spain. I left Santa Maria at 2 o'clock in the morning in order to arrive at Barcelona in the early afternoon. I climbed up to 9000 feet (FL090) and trimmed up the airplane for cruise. In the rather dim lights of the Sundowner, what instruments I could see indicated that everything was normal; so in due course I gave Santa Maria my first position report and estimate of the next and settled down for the long flight ahead.

A few minutes later I realized that the lights were definitely fading. With my trusty flashlight, I looked at the ammeter down on the bottom of the panel, and to my horror it was showing complete discharge. Ouch! Immediately I called Santa Maria and told them that I was returning, that my alternator was out of service, and that I would have to turn off all my radios. I expected to be back in their vicinity in about 45 minutes, at which time I would attempt to contact them for landing instructions. However, if that proved impossible, would they please give me a light for landing. They agreed to this and asked if I was declaring an emergency. I replied that I did not expect an emergency but was not sure how long the battery would last for communicating.

Fortunately it was a beautiful clear night, with no clouds even over the islands, so the light beacon up on the mountain could be seen for a long way out. I turned off everything except the flashlight and thanked my Guardian Angel for being prompt in warning me of trouble. The landing gear was, of course, fixed, so that was not a problem, and when I got closer in, the battery still was strong enough to communicate for a normal approach, although I did leave the landing light off.

Later in the morning when the mechanic for the local airline came to work and looked at the alternator, he discovered that all the wires had broken at their connectors. He repaired them, and I left again that night without further incident. When I got home, I immediately invested in my Lamar Volt Monitor and have not been without it since.

My Guardian Angel was right on the job, but a friend of mine had a somewhat less alert Guardian Angel in the same circumstances when he was delivering an agricultural airplane.

We had met in Santa Maria. I had a Baron for Madrid, and he was taking the ag plane to Africa, so we decided to have dinner together at a special place he knew in Madrid the following night. He left long before I did, having a slow airplane, but there was no sign of him when I arrived in Madrid. I waited and waited, but in vain.

The next time I saw him, he told me that his alternator had gone to pieces, but he didn't know it until his ADF went dead and his communication radio was suspiciously silent. It was dark by this time, and so with no navigation aid of any kind, and only his flashlight to see with, he waited for the coast of the Iberian Peninsula to show up and hoped he would recognize where he was. When he did come to it, his Guardian Angel woke up and told him to turn south to Lisbon, which he did, and he finally got into Lisbon all unbeknownst to the tower, with no lights and no radio. He was there for many days waiting for a new alternator from the States. I gave him a volt monitor for Christmas, which was coming up, and he also uses it all the time. One lesson is usually enough for most of us.

If things like this can happen in a new airplane, there is no reason to think they cannot happen in an older one. So investigate the health of your electrical system and invest in an early-warning gadget.

If your engine can pass muster in all these areas and its accessories can too, it should be quite safe for an ocean flight whether you have one or two.

5 Emergency Equipment

The amount and variety of emergency equipment you carry will depend largely on your imagining of what you may need and your belief in the efficacy of emergency equipment in general. There is a minimum which must be carried:

Life raft to accommodate all occupants of the aircraft
Life vests for each occupant
Emergency transmitter which is portable and waterproof
Flares and signaling devices

Beyond these basic items there are such things as water bottles, food rations, fishing tackle, oars, sails, water distillers, patching kits for the raft, etc.

There is a place on the International Flight Plan Form for the listing of the emergency equipment, and in theory your airplane may be examined at any departure point to be sure the equipment is there and available.

If you are flying a single-engine airplane and departing from a Canadian airport, you must stop at Moncton, New Brunswick, so the Canadian Department of Transport Inspector can check the airplane and its equipment as well as the knowledge and experience of the pilot. This is the only situation in which an inspection is sure.

If you do not wish to buy this equipment, there are places where it is possible to rent it for the trip. Most of these rentals are to be found in the Fort Lauderdale, Florida, area, which is the main departure point for flights to the Caribbean Islands.

Perhaps I am a pessimist, but I have little faith in my ability to ditch an airplane in the rough water of the North Atlantic successfully enough to get the door open, the life raft out and inflated, and myself into it before I freeze to death in water the temperature of which limits one's life expectancy to 1 to 3 minutes. I am not even sure of the survivability of the Pacific.

It is true that over the years since men first started trying to fly across the ocean there have been occasional intrepid aviators who were saved when they had to ditch, but this is so rare that I hardly think of it as a probability.

In October 1910, Captain Walter Wellman planned to make the first crossing to Europe in his airship *America*. He encountered bad weather and engine problems and was blown badly off course but, fortunately for him, to the South. I was unaware that there were radios in those days, but the book says he had a radio on which he sent out an SOS. He also had a life boat attached to the bottom of his gondola. The freighter S.S. *Trent* heard his call and steamed toward his reported position, so when the crew had to abandon the *America* and take to the lifeboat, S.S. *Trent* was right there and picked them all up after a 3-hour struggle with the rough sea. They were 400 miles east of Cape Hatteras.

In May 1919, Hawker and Grieve ditched alongside the Danish cargo boat S.S. *Mary* on their attempted first flight across the North Atlantic. The *Mary* picked them up and all was well, although the *Mary* did not have radio, so it was several days later before the world knew that they were safe.

Stanley Haussner started from New Jersey to fly nonstop to his native Poland in his high-wing Bellanca, in June 1932. His plans had been very carefully made, but what he did not expect happened. His fuel tanks began to leak when he was more than halfway across, with the result that he had to ditch in the dark. He must have been a good pilot because he succeeded and the airplane floated. He had no raft, and he survived in the airplane and on its wing for 7 days. Finally, when he was at the end of his strength from starvation and thirst, the S.S. *Cire Shell* spotted him and rescued him more dead than alive; he was 600 miles from the French coast.

On the other hand, there was a husband-and-wife team just a few years ago who missed the Azores completely and ran out of fuel about 300 miles off the coast of Portugal. They ditched near a Rumanian fishing vessel, which later reported having seen them wave, but they were not picked up.

Inevitably, with as much traffic as there is across all the oceans, there have been a few lost in most years, and once in a great while one who is rescued.

My personal belief that emergency equipment is only a morale builder was reinforced in April 1966. I was delivering an airplane whose oil cooler was on the front of the engine just behind the propeller. The factory supplied baffle was not available for this airplane, so, knowing how cold the air is in the North in April, I had taped over the central section of the cooler. Just after I passed Ocean Station Charlie and my point of no return, the oil temperature rose to the red line and the oil pressure dropped to its red line. I could not account for this, so decided to return to "Charlie" in case I had to ditch; I also reduced the power to about 45 percent.

As soon as I called "Charlie" to tell him I was returning and why, he sent out a request for Air-Sea Rescue to both

Gander and Prestwick, Scotland, and also told everybody on the frequency to keep quiet as he had an emergency. You could almost hear the heavy breathing as all the airplanes within several hundred miles listened to every word that "Charlie" or I said. When I was back over him, I suggested that he call off Search and Rescue, and circled over him for about 20 minutes trying to decide what was wrong and whether I would really have to ditch.

Finally a TWA flight couldn't stand the suspense and asked, "What seems to be your problem?"

When I said that my oil was too hot and had practically no pressure and he said, "Why don't you come up here where it is cool, about minus fifty degrees?"

With that, the light dawned! Of course, it was cold where I was, and the tape was not keeping the oil from congealing in the cooler. What I needed was to go down to warmer air, if any. I asked "Charlie" what the surface temperature was and he said, "Forty-five degrees." So down into the clouds I went, and at about 2000 feet the oil in the cooler began to circulate and the pressure began to rise. I thanked TWA for sparking my realization of the problem, assured everybody that the emergency was over, and told "Charlie" that I would proceed on course to Shannon.

The Gander Search plane had already gone home, but the Prestwick one felt he should find me in case of further trouble. The only thing was that his Direction Finding (DF) equipment was out of service so he could only go by what I reported as a position, which of course was not all that accurate. He sent out flares, but I could not find them; in due course night came on, and we both turned on all our lights, but without success. It was not until we were both on Ocean Station Juliet's radar that she could steer him to me. I was underneath a layer of clouds which he was on top of, so our lights had no chance. Once he found me, he put out his landing gear, flaps, and spoilers to "dirty" up the airplane so he could maintain as slow a speed as my lordly 130 knots. He stayed with me right to the airport at Shannon.

The point of the story is this. Suppose that instead of being in the air, with at least a fair idea of where I was and able to communicate until "Juliet" found us, I had had to ditch somewhere. Without his DF equipment the Prestwick plane was blind, and the ocean was completely cloud-covered; a raft is, in any case, a very small object, especially at night. What chance would I have had? And now, of course, neither Ocean Station Charlie nor Juliet is there any more with their radar.

However, I don't know any other ferry pilot who has my cynical attitude toward such a possibility. They all carry emergency equipment quite happily, and indeed are insulted when it is suggested that the equipment is nothing but excess baggage.

One piece of emergency equipment which I find invaluable, and so far, always available when I need it is my Guardian Angel.

The night I lost my ADF enroute to Santa Maria lives in my memory as proof that no matter how careful one is, there are times when one's Guardian Angel plays a large part in the success of an ocean flight. This was in the days when the Coast Guard Ocean Station Vessels were stationed on all North Atlantic routes.

As is usual, the ADF had been carefully checked from Wichita to Norwood, Massachusetts, and was working well although I thought it hadn't quite the range I would like. There was, however, nothing to really complain about. When I left Boston for Yarmouth, Nova Scotia, 235 nautical miles away, the needle pointed firmly and steadily from about 160 miles out, so I was satisfied.

From Gander to Santa Maria, one proceeds South to overhead Torbay, Newfoundland, and from there straight out to Ocean Station Delta, whose on-station position was 540 nautical miles southeast of Newfoundland toward the Azores. I stayed on the outbound radial of St. John's VOR until my needle flagged at about 90 miles out at 9000 feet. The drift correction to hold this radial confirmed my flight-plan drift correction, so it was simply a matter of holding the same heading until the needle was ready to point at "Delta," which normally would be 150 miles before arriving over her. I could plan to talk to her at about 100 miles out, and she would get me on her radar at about 90 miles. My estimated groundspeed was 150 knots, so there were 2 hours to just hold heading and wait. At 9000 feet the air was smooth, the sun was shining, and there was only a very low broken cloud layer over the water. With little visual reference to indicate speed in these conditions, it seems that you and the airplane are one entity suspended in illimitable space; a time when the cares and frustrations of life on the ground seem very far away, and peace prevails in mind and body.

The time came when "Delta's" beacon should be calling my ADF needle, but nothing happened and it was still aimlessly circling the dial. For 20 minutes I worked with the tuner to get exactly on frequency. Finally about 100 miles from "Delta," the needle began to answer her and point. I tried to call.

"Ocean Station Delta, do you read Sacchi 86 on one two six decimal seven?"

"Sacchi 86, this is Delta—reading you loud and clear, go ahead your message."

"OK, Delta. Sacchi 86 is a BE33, departed Gander at ten twenty Zulu, destination Santa Maria at twenty forty Zulu, last reported position four five three zero North and four five West at one three two five, flight level nine zero, estimating your on-station position at one four four five. Would appreciate a position and a track and groundspeed check when you have me on your radar."

"Delta copied all; what is your present position?"

"I'm bearing two nine five from you and should be about ninety-five miles."

"We're looking. . . . Sacchi 86 from Delta, we have you now eight-seven miles on bearing two hundred ninety-six;

stand by for track and groundspeed. Meanwhile, could you send some messages for us?"

"86—sure will; go ahead."

"OK here's the first. Mrs. J. A. Miller, 4234 Main Street, Terrell, Texas. How copy?"

"Got it all, go ahead."

"Dear Mom, just want you to know I am OK and thinking of you. Take care and give my love to Dot. Your loving son, Jim."

"OK all copied, who's next?"

"This one goes to Miss Delores Farrell, Box 576, Canterbury (I spell, charlie, alpha, november, tango, echo, romeo, bravo, uniform, romeo, yankee), Pennsylvania."

"Copied, go ahead."

"Darling, I miss you, will be home in two weeks, love Frank. How copy?"

"Copied OK."

"We have just one more if you don't mind."

"No, glad to send them, go."

"Thanks, this is to Miss Gladys James, 1525 Water Street, Plymouth, Massachusetts. OK?"

"Was that Water or Walter?"

"It's water like the ocean."

"OK, go ahead."

"Gladys darling, your honey misses you like crazy, hope you miss me too, see you soon, all my love, Frank."

"86 has them all. Frank must be one of those proverbial sailors with a girl in every port!"

"This time he is innocent of the charge, we have two Franks. Thanks a lot, and we have a track and groundspeed if you are ready to copy."

"Go ahead."

"We have you tracking one hundred twenty degrees at speed of two hundred sixty knots, how does that check?"

"Wow, it sure would be nice but I'd need about a hundred knot tailwind."

"Sorry, we'll try again. What is a B33, we thought you were a jet?"

"It's a BE33 and I'm a single-engine Bonanza that cruises at one hundred forty knots."

"Oh, only one engine? You're brave to go all that distance in such an airplane."

"Not really, it's safer than driving any day. How is your weather down there today?"

"It's great, everybody is out taking a sunbath."

"I think I will take a picture of you as I go by; hardly ever see you down there. Got a new groundspeed yet?"

"Affirmative, this time we make it one hundred fifty knots, how is that?"

"That is about what I figured so I should be on time over you."

This type of conversation could go on for an hour or more as one approached, and went away from the ship. It was pleasant for them and for us, and I think most of the passing airplanes sent messages for them, so their families heard from them from odd spots in the world, and I at least, always got a kick out of putting these messages on postcards and sending them to strange women. I did take a picture, and there was somebody on deck waving something white at me.

Since an ADF back bearing on the ship's beacon could not be counted on for more than about 30 miles, I did not worry when I lost it. They gave me a couple more positions before I flew off their radar screen, so I knew that I was on course for Flores Island, which is the first landfall in the Azores. The Flores NDB was not very strong, but at that time there was a very powerful NDB at the Lajes Air Base, which is a combined United States–Portugal Base.

As one always does when one is past the halfway point, I was trying to hurry things and tuned in Lajes as soon as I lost "Delta's" beacon. Since I was still more than 600 miles from Lajes, of course nothing happened; but even when I should have been able to reach Lajes, there was still nothing. No matter how I tuned the receiver, the needle continued to circle aimlessly, and there was nothing but noise in the receiver; finally I had to admit that the ADF was really useless and I needed my Guardian Angel to find the islands for me. If I succeeded in getting close enough, both Lajes and Santa Maria have a VOR which could bring me in, but first I had to arrive in their vicinity by holding tight to my flight-plan heading at least until my Flores estimate. Meanwhile it was getting dark. At the prescribed times I called Santa Maria to tell them where I was, at least, where I hoped I was. The islands are usually covered with clouds, so I wondered whether there was any chance of seeing the light beacon on Flores to give me a position. I kept a sharp watch for a possible break in the clouds, and as you can imagine, a constant check on the time, which seemed to pass very slowly.

A light flashes down there! Is it Flores? A fishing boat? What? There, it was coming again—and again. It must be Flores because my time indicated that I should arrive over Flores in 5 more minutes.

The longer I watched the surer I was that it was Flores, so I called Santa Maria and told them I was at Flores and set the new course for Gracioso, which is the next island. Just before Gracioso the VOR came to life on Lajes, and the rest was all a piece of cake into Santa Maria.

After that experience, I never had any qualms about making a landfall at night, because I believe that in the daytime I might have missed the island under the clouds.

I try not to overwork my Guardian Angel, but it is nice to know that he is there when I need him, and much more useful than a life raft.

6

The Magnetic Compass

The Magnetic Compass has been the basic navigation instrument for untold centuries. There is some reason to believe that I had some familiarity with it about 12,000 years ago, in a lifetime in Atlantis. That civilization died out, and about 5000 years later in the Eastern Mediterranean, in another lifetime, I reinvented it. However, that civilization also died, and its knowledge was lost. In the thirteenth century the fact that the earth has a magnetic field which can be used with a magnet in a ship was rediscovered. This information was used to direct a ship in its sailing across the seas of the then known world. With some refinements, the basic concept is still used in ships and aircraft for navigating on the surface of the earth, in the skies above, and in the seas below the surface.

Except near the North Pole, where we are so close to the earth's magnetic field that the vertical tilt overcomes the horizontal directional force, this little gem will always tell us in which direction we are proceeding, as long as we make allowance for its foibles.

CHARACTERISTICS

The Magnetic Compass is, of course, a magnet. The earth has a large magnetic field at 76°N100°W on Bathurst Island, approximately 840 nautical miles South of the *True* North Pole. The compass magnet points at all times to this Magnetic North Pole and not to the *True* North Pole. All navigation charts have lines on them which tell us the angle between this Magnetic North and the *True* North from whatever position we find ourselves. These are called *Isogonic lines* and are lines of equal Variation. Since the earth's magnetic field changes its position slightly from year to year, in relation to *True* North, the lines of Variation must also change slightly from year to year. This is noted on charts as they are printed. Since Sir James Clark Ross located the magnetic pole in 1831, it has migrated 350 nautical miles North-northwest.

From some parts of the world the Magnetic Pole will lie to the West of the *True* pole, so we must add the value of the angle to our *True* heading to compensate for the fact that the magnetic compass will point further West than *True* North. From other parts of the world, the Magnetic North lies to the East of *True* North, and so the angle must be subtracted. There are also two lines where the Magnetic and *True* North are exactly lined up and the Variation will be zero. These are called *Agonic lines*.

Since the Magnetic Compass is a magnet, it will also be attracted to any magnetic material in the airplane in which it is mounted. Electrically induced magnetic fields from radios, lights, etc., also set up a magnetic field to which it will respond. Sometimes these two sources combine to cause quite large errors in the compass reading. We call this disturbance *Deviation* and attempt to minimize its effect by compensating the compass with the use of two small magnets in the compass base.

It is seldom possible to eliminate entirely this error of Deviation, so a card is prepared to denote the remainder which must be allowed for on each heading.

SWINGING AND COMPENSATING A COMPASS

Figure 6-1 shows the compass face and the screws for the two adjusting magnets. Figure 6-2 shows a typical airport Compass Rose, which is painted on a surface away from any buildings or other source of magnetic disturbance and is oriented to Magnetic North.

With the engine running at a high enough rpm to have the alternator/generator operating and the vacuum or pressure pump for the gyro instruments up to speed:

1. Line up the airplane on the Compass Rose and pointing North. This is easier if there is someone outside to direct us. The airplane should be as nearly as possible in flying position, which is easy with a tricycle-gear airplane, but one with a tail wheel must be supported in flying position. A

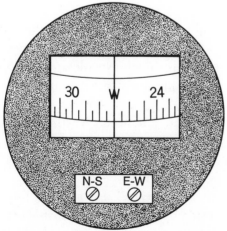

FIGURE 6-1
The face and adjusting screws of a Magnetic Compass.

sawhorse is handy for this; of course, the helper outside gets a good dose of wind from the prop each time we change direction.

2. Now see what the compass reads with all the radios turned on. Be sure there are no magnetic screws or tools in

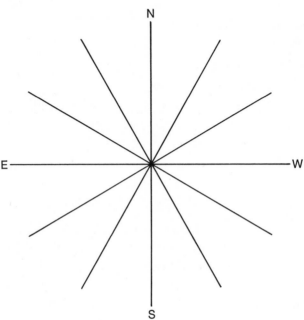

FIGURE 6-2
An airport Compass Rose.

its vicinity. That injunction is not as silly as it sounds; I once had a series of new airplanes which had steel screws holding the compass to the glareshield. Needless to say, until they were removed, the compass would point only at those screws.

3. If there is a difference between North on the Compass Rose and what your compass reads, take a brass screwdriver (be sure it is brass) and on the screw marked North-South adjust the reading to North.

4. Now turn the airplane to East on the Compass Rose and remove any error by adjusting the East-West screw.

5. Turn the airplane to South. If you are lucky, there will

be no error on this heading. If there is, for example, it reads 184°, remove one half of the error with the North-South screw.

6. Turn the airplane to West. If there is an error, remove one half of it with the East-West screw.

Now your compass is compensated to the extent this is possible.

Whatever error is left—the smaller the better—you must live with, but you do want to know exactly how much it is on all headings, and they won't all be the same. Get out your pencil and paper; turn back to North and write down the compass reading. Do this every 30° all the way around the circle and you have a way to allow for any error caused by the airplane and its components.

If you plan to do a lot of cross-country flying at night, it is wise to go through the same swing and note the error on each 30° with the cockpit and navigation and rotating beacon lights on. Not the landing light, as you only use that in the vicinity of an airport.

Your final correction card will look like this:

Day		Night	
N = 002	S = 181	N = 359	S = 178
030 = 031	210 = 210	030 = 028	210 = 207
060 = 060	240 = 241	060 = 059	240 = 239
E = 089	W = 269	E = 088	W = 267
120 = 119	300 = 302	120 = 123	300 = 304
150 = 152	330 = 328	150 = 152	330 = 327

As you can see, this compass compensated nearly perfectly; in fact, when one considers that an average pilot cannot hold a heading closer than 3°, there is hardly any correction to make. Not all compasses will come out this well, but it is a big advantage in ocean flying when the compass will compensate closely.

In the course of quite a few formation flights across the

North Atlantic I have discovered that if all our compasses have been compensated accurately, we have had no trouble arriving at the same place even when we were out of sight of each other for some hours. I could say, "Let's hold 110°," the others would follow, and sooner or later we would find ourselves together.

The first time it happened, a new pilot was flying the other plane. We were supposed to form up over Wesleyville, but neither of us could see the other. I just told him each time I changed heading and tried harder than usual to hold the heading exactly, as did he. The airplanes were identical, and we were using the same power settings. It was winter so night came a little more than halfway across, and all of a sudden he jubilantly announced, "I see your beacon right in front of me about two miles!" While this seemed uncanny at the time, it happened so often afterward that I became even more of a firm believer in really accurate compensation of the compass.

AGE AND CONDITION

If the compass is fairly old, it could be a good idea to have it checked by an instrument shop. If the fluid level is low or the pivot on which the card rotates is worn, any inaccuracies will be exaggerated when you get into the higher latitudes of the North Atlantic routes to Europe. The angle of Variation increases up to 40° West in the vicinity of Northern Canada and Greenland, so the magnet dips quite a bit to point to Magnetic North, which means that it already has a tendency to stick, even if fluid and pivot are as they should be.

A friend of mine has recently come back from a trip through the Caribbean and Central America. She had some trouble with her navigation because her compass kept leaking, and without fluid to float in and relieve the pressure on the pivot, the compass will get stuck. Although the airplane changes its direction, the compass does not follow.

You can easily see what this can led to where there are no landmarks to steer by.

TURNING AND ACCELERATION ERRORS

Because of the pivot the compass has some errors.

Northerly Turning Error

On Northerly headings, a turn toward either East or West will cause the compass card to go in the opposite direction to the turn, and it will catch up with the new heading only when the airplane is again straight and level on the new heading. On Southerly headings, in a turn toward East or West, the compass card will be in a hurry and run ahead of the turn, only settling back when the airplane is straight and level on the new heading.

Acceleration Errors

Acceleration errors occur on Easterly and Westerly headings when the aircraft speed is increased or decreased, either by a change of throttle setting or by climbing or descending. When you do any of these things, the compass will point as much as 20° to one side or the other of your actual heading. The only time it is accurate is when the airplane is level both horizontally and longitudinally. This is the only time to reset your gyro.

Position Errors

When you take a Northern Hemisphere compass into the Southern Hemisphere without recompensating it, as when you go to Australia or New Zealand, another thing can happen to it, presumably because of the position of the Magnetic South Pole at approximately 69°S139°E, which is moving 8 nautical miles Northwest each year. It can read as much as 25° too high on Westerly and low on Easterly headings.

I was quite surprised on my first trip to Australia to discover that in order to track in to Auckland, New Zealand, with my ADF I had what appeared to be about 25° more drift correction than I had expected from the forecast wind. It wasn't until I happened to notice that my heading did not at all agree with the runway heading on landing that it came to me what was probably the reason for that odd drift. Uncorrected, this much error could well lead a person to miss land entirely and head off to the South Pole. Embarrassing!

ANCILLARY COMPASSES

Many airplanes have another kind of Magnetic Compass, in which the magnet is remote from the fuselage and its disturbances; usually it is out in the wing. Only the dial is on the panel; this compass is compensated when it is installed, and its calibration is frequently perfect. It is also less subject to turning errors and acceleration errors and is impervious to the addition and subtraction of radios or other equipment in the cockpit.

The directional gyro is one way we avoid trying to fly an accurate heading by outguessing the flighty gyrations of the Magnetic Compass. However, the directional gyro has its own problems, chiefly that because it is a gyro spinning (somewhat like a top) and the earth is also spinning at a different rate, the gyro precesses, or goes off heading. The rate of precession should not be more than 3° per 15 minutes. If it is, better overhaul the gyro or get a new one before you start across the ocean. Also, unless the compass is stable and level when you reset the gyro, there is another error.

The Magnetic Compass is, in any environment, the basic navigational instrument; we even find them in the most advanced airline aircraft, just in case. It is also the simplest instrument and the one requiring the least maintenance. If we give it what little it does need and then trust what it tells us after making allowances for its inherent foibles, it will always be a faithful friend to any navigator.

7
The Charts

The world is round (almost) and paper is flat, so chart-makers have some compromising to do in order to project this round world onto a flat paper. They have, over the centuries, come up with several different methods of doing this, and these are called *projections*. Basically, we have Mercator, Lambert, and Stereographic projections.

*   *   *

Figure 7-1 is a Mercator projection, which was the first one to see wide use. It was invented in 1586 by Gerhardus Mercator, who was a Flemish geographer and mathematician. Since we still use it essentially unchanged, Mercator must have been a pretty smart man. What he did was to wrap a sheet of paper around the globe, tangent to the surface at the equator, with the source of projection at the imaginary center of the globe. This means that at the equator the scale is exact and becomes more distorted (enlarged) the further toward the poles you look. On this chart all the meridians of longitude (East-West) are parallel lines, and all the parallels of latitude (North-South), as their name implies, are also parallel lines. They cross the meridians at a 90° angle.

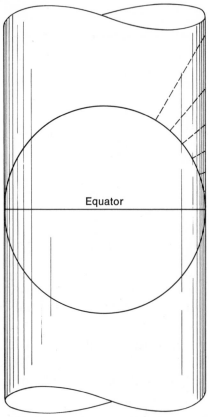

FIGURE 7-1
Mercator projection.

On the real world all the meridians converge at the Poles, so Mercator's chart gives Greenland, Siberia, Alaska, and Antarctica an unfair advantage in size over the rest of us.

*   *   *

Figure 7-2 shows a Lambert Conformal Conic projection. This was named for its original inventor, Johann Heinrich Lambert (1728–1777), who was an Alsatian navigator. As it was a more accurate representation of the midlatitudes, it was adopted by the allies in World War I. It is called *confor-*

mal because it conforms fairly well to the shape of the globe and *conic* because the projection is based on a cone. That is logical, I guess.

This cone is tangent to the globe at any two parallels of latitude, perhaps 33 and 45° North (or South), or it could be any other convenient pair of latitudes, such as 36 and 60° North, or whatever you like.

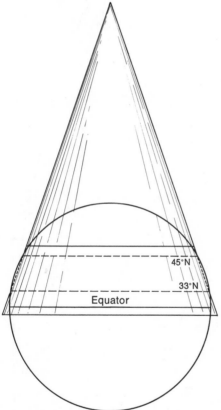

FIGURE 7-2
Lambert Conformal Conic projection.

On these two parallels the scale is exact; between them the globe surface is squeezed a bit to flatten it out onto the paper, and beyond the two parallels the surface is expanded a bit to flatten it out. However, to all intents and purposes, the Lambert chart is as accurate as is possible, and a straight line plotted on it is essentially a Great Circle (Figure 7-3*a*),

FIGURE 7-3

Part of a Lambert chart. (a) A Great Circle route and a Rhumb Line have been plotted. (b) The chart has been cut and separated along the meridians to make it the equivalent of a Mercator projection. Now the Great Circle route, which was straight, becomes curved. The Rhumb Line, which was curved on the Lambert projection, becomes straight.

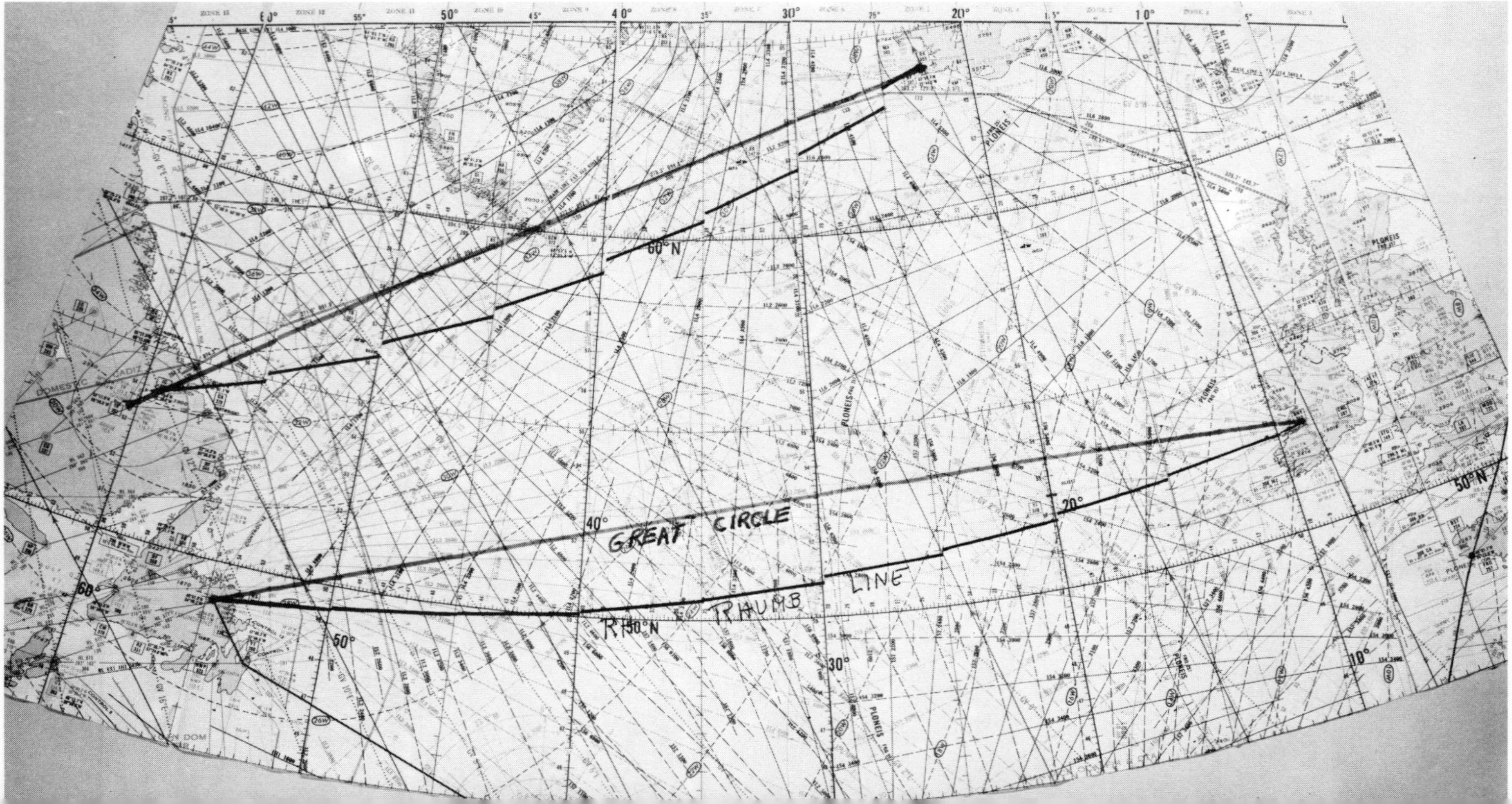

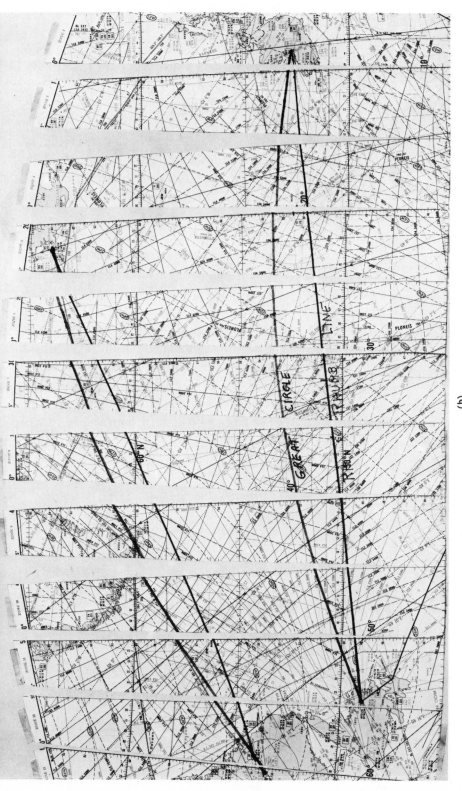

(b)

which is the shortest distance between any two points on the earth. This track crosses each meridian at a different angle because of the convergence of the meridians. On the Mercator chart, because the meridians are parallel lines, the Great Circle track must be a curved line. On the other hand, a rhumb-line track, which is used more in sailing, is a straight line on the Mercator and a curved line on the Lambert (Figure 7-3*b*), because the rhumb-line track uses a constant heading and therefore will cross all meridians at the same angle.

*   *   *

Figure 7-4 shows a Polar Stereographic projection. I don't know who invented this one, but it is accomplished by placing a piece of paper tangent to the globe at one of the Poles, backing off to the other Pole and projecting from there through the center of the globe, in a North-South direction. The result of this is that the parallels of latitude come out as concentric circles around the pole and the meridians of longitude look like the spokes of a wheel. The scale accuracy deteriorates as you get further away from the Pole, so it is used for Polar navigation. Here too, a Great Circle is a straight line.

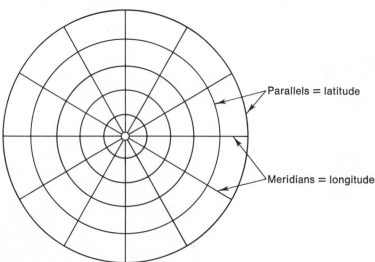

Parallels = latitude

Meridians = longitude

FIGURE 7-4
Polar Stereographic projection.

The charts used for air navigation over great distances are frequently a combination of these different types of projections. The Aircraft Position Charts 3071 and 3097, which we use for crossing the North Atlantic, are Lambert Conformal Conic; therefore, a straight line is a Great Circle track and crosses each meridian at a different angle.

On these charts, distance is measured up and down a meridian, and 1 nautical mile equals 1 minute of latitude, or, to say it another way, 60 nautical miles equals 1 degree of latitude as there are 60 minutes in 1 degree. Nautical miles are the standard of measure for navigation because of this fact. Aircraft Position Charts are available with or without Loran information; they provide information on oceanic control areas, flight information regions, topographic information such as spot elevations, important drainage features, large cities, and international boundaries.

When working out and filing an ICAO flight plan, you must take into consideration the position of the oceanic control area and flight information region boundaries, because they are required position reporting points.

$$*   *   *$$

For portions of the flight which are over land, either islands or continents, I also like to carry ONC (operational navigation charts). Since they are on the same scale as our WAC (world aeronautic charts), there is considerably more of both topography and culture on them. They are twice as big as our WACs, which can make them awkward in the cockpit, but my problem is that I am always curious about where I am. I like to know what that town, or river, or mountain, or chateau is and where that highway or railroad or canal goes. For this kind of geographical curiosity one needs a chart on a 1:1,000,000 scale rather than the 1:5,000,000 of the Aircraft Position Chart.

$$*   *   *$$

Another type of chart which is necessary for any foreign flying is the Enroute Low (or High) Altitude Radio Facility

Charts, and their associated Supplement, and the Low Altitude Instrument Approach Charts. You may not intend to do any instrument flying, but it is certainly well to be prepared in case you get caught by bad weather; weather in Europe is as unpredictable as it is here, sometimes I think even worse than here.

The Radio Facility charts can be had either from Jeppesen Company or the Department of Commerce. I started out using the Department of Commerce ones because they were cheaper (I think they are not any more), and they had the advantage for a lazy pilot that the revisions come all at once in a new book, instead of requiring you to change sheet by sheet every week, as with Jeppesen. However, I discovered one day that not all the airports one may want are included. Because I had used the Geneva, Switzerland, plate many times, I assumed that there was also an approach plate for Zurich without ever checking to make sure. One day my destination airport, which was Munich, fell flat when I was nearing Zurich, so I announced to Zurich Approach that I would like to come in. He cleared me for an ILS approach to Runway 13; I acknowledged happily and pulled out the Volume 2 Approach plate book to find Zurich. To my horror, there was no Zurich! How could that be? I reached for the Supplement; at least that would have frequencies in it, if it had Zurich at all, only to discover that I had put it away in the suitcase behind the tanks at Shannon. Foolishly, I had thought I would not need it any more because I knew the Shannon-Munich route by heart. This thought can come under the heading of "famous last words" in some circumstances.

Anyway, there I was, and Controllers do not like people who come into their area in bad weather without proper information. So I called, "Zurich Approach, can you confirm the localizer frequency for Runway 13, please? My needle is not indicating."

He came back with the frequency, and "do you have a localizer receiver?" I assured him I had, and perhaps I was still too far out. A few minutes later, I called him back to say that my needle was now indicating normally on the localizer. Fortunately, although the weather was bad, it was not nearly down to minimums, so I had no trouble with the approach even though I had never been into Zurich before.

*   *   *

You can believe that as soon as I had attended to the required visits with Customs and Immigration personnel, I sought out the local charter operator, begged a copy of the approaches for Zurich, and carried them with me ever after. Never again did I put anything in the way of charts or Supplement out of reach until I had arrived at my final destination.

8
The Weather

The importance of a good basic knowledge of weather and how to fly it cannot be overemphasized. It can and often does spell the difference between success and failure in any ocean-flying attempt.

By good basic knowledge I mean the ability, which comes only with practice, to interpret the weather charts and satellite pictures, to correlate the current weather sequences with the forecasts, and to ask intelligent questions of the forecaster/briefer. These questions must get right down to the nitty-gritty of the information to give you an intelligent basis for deciding whether to go or wait for another day.

*   *   *

We are all aware that since the Weather Bureau has been depending entirely on their computers and the individual Weather Offices no longer draw their own weather maps, the quality of the forecasts we receive has deteriorated markedly. This of course, is not the fault of the individual

Weather Station. Although they have a plethora of data from the computers, there is not as much pertinent information available as there once was, especially in the lower levels, in which the computer programmers apparently have no interest.

Also, and unfortunately, year by year there are fewer forecaster/briefers; those who are left have so many extraneous duties that they cannot pay as much attention to aviation weather problems as they used to or as they would like to. If the briefer gives a forecast which is different from the official one, he is sticking his neck way out, even though he is reasonably sure that the official forecast is probably wrong.

Most of the larger Weather Stations have equipment to gather the satellite pictures, but due to "lack of man power" they frequently do not turn on the machine; so here we have a valuable source of information going to waste at great expense to the taxpayer who spent a great deal of money to put the satellite in orbit. Satellite pictures have become even more important because of the computers; when you can find one, it has much valuable information. All the clouds are there, although you will need a forecaster trained to interpret the various shades of white into the types of clouds and their height. Low Pressure Centers and Fronts show up clearly, and where the winds are strong one can also see the direction.

The satellite picture should be compared with what is called the Significant Weather Chart. This purports to show the significant weather from the surface up to 20,000 feet. Since the weather is seldom the same all the way up through this much altitude, it is largely a matter of guesswork whether the chart is depicting the weather near the surface or further up in the atmosphere. By comparing the chart and the satellite picture one can make a more intelligent guess as to the situation pertaining to the altitude which is of interest—tops of clouds, density of clouds, etc.

*   *   *

If you spend some time with the forecasters in the Gander, Newfoundland, Weather Office before leaving for Greenland, or any other trans-Atlantic destination, you will learn much. They are the best forecasters for the lower levels over the ocean because they have many years of experience in this type of forecasting, and just as important, they are truly interested in the problems of the light-plane pilot. Unfortunately, the Gander forecasters too must depend on the computers for much of their information. However, they still draw their own weather charts and incorporate whatever reports are available from ships and aircraft which are crossing the ocean.

Before computers, and when the eight Weather Ships were stationed at various points around the North Atlantic to send wind and weather information to shore stations on both sides of the ocean, a Gander forecast was about 95 percent accurate for the ocean crossing.

Figure 8-1 shows the North Atlantic basin as it was before 1973, when there were the eight Ocean Station Vessels reporting wind and weather. If you cross off those eight vessels, you can easily see how much of the forecasting for the ocean area must be pure guesswork. In addition to guessing the weather, the forecasters must now also guess the wind direction and velocity. With only the four points around the edge giving upper winds, there can be no certainty of the direction and velocity in the large expanses of ocean between them. These ships were removed by the United States and the European countries in the name of "economy" and because "they were no longer needed."

$$*\qquad*\qquad*$$

That the Gander forecasters still worry about us was brought home to me when, after a particularly bad trip through unforecast weather, I sent back a postcard with a description of the wind and weather encountered with the rather plaintive question,"Are you trying to get rid of me?"

The next week when I went through Gander again, they had made up self-addressed postcards with mimeographed

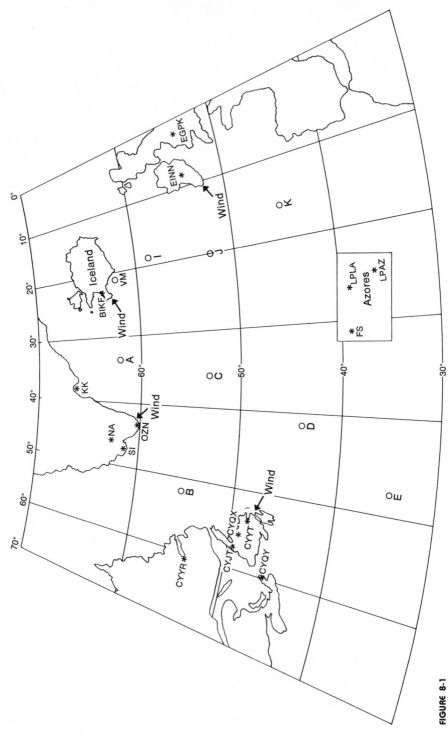

FIGURE 8-1
North Atlantic Ocean Station Vessels. Stations B to E were
United States stations, and A and I to K were European.

headings to report the comparison between the forecast and actual wind and weather; these were given to every pilot leaving for Europe. When the card was returned, the forecasters kept it and compared it with their charts, and I believe we all benefited.

$$*\qquad*\qquad*$$

The trip which occasioned this postcard was one on which I was supposed to be on the South side of a Low Pressure Center with a fairly decent tailwind until I crossed the weak front about two-thirds of the way across, after which the wind would be from the South and of little help. All went well until I was almost two-thirds across and could no longer turn back. My Loran indicated that the tailwind was not as good as forecast but nothing to worry about. Then I hit the weather, and the situation rapidly deteriorated. I considered the turbulence moderate and occasionally severe; the precipitation was heavy; the OAT dropped from $+1$ to $-1°C$, so it soon turned to ice. This situation requires a change of altitude, the question to be decided being: Shall I go up or down? The turbulence and precipitation, plus the fact that the clouds were solid rather than fuzzy and the light inside them fairly dim, indicated to me that the tops would be quite high and out of my reach without oxygen. I elected to go down. From my cruising altitude of 9000 feet down to 4000 feet the temperature did not change (one frequently finds this isothermal condition over the ocean), but when I got to 3000 feet the temperature was up to $+1°C$ again, and the ice slowly started to come off. Naturally, in this type of weather the Loran was all "grass," the ADF needle went round and round, and the HF was only loud static. Knowing nothing of the direction and velocity of the wind at this altitude, except that it was undoubtedly not helpful, the only thing to do was try to hold my precomputed heading and hope for the best. There was no autopilot on this airplane, so it was hard work to hold something near the desired heading in the turbulence. This was one of the times when you say to yourself "there must be easier ways to earn a living!" Luckily, Ocean Station Juliet, which was the last one to be decomissioned, was still in her position at 52°30′N20°W. From 9000 feet, one could talk to her about 100 nautical miles away, but from 3000 feet, my range was only about 45 miles. Some minutes after I should have passed her, I finally was able to get an answer to my calls; she got me on her radar and my position was not too far off course, but my speed was horrifying. She had no cheerful news about when I would be out of the weather except that the Shannon forecast was fairly good. Since I had lost 40 minutes in the last 300 miles, I re-estimated Shannon figuring to lose another hour in that 400 miles, and "Juliet" relayed my new estimate to them. I said a devout "Thank You" to "Juliet" and also thanked my lucky stars for the ample fuel reserve of my single-engine airplane.

At about 15° West the temperature rose fairly rapidly, which indicated a shift of the wind to the South, so I climbed back up to my assigned altitude of 9000 feet. Although it was now dark, I was delighted to discover that I was mostly on top with bright stars and the moon just rising. Now I would be able to receive the Eagle and Shannon VORs and to talk to Shannon on VHF at the expected distance.

After I landed I went to the Met Office to see what had happened to my forecast weather and wind. The Low Pressure Center which had been expected to lie slightly to the North of track had drifted to the East and South, so I had spent 4 hours in its North and East quadrants with the worst weather and most adverse winds.

This was a rather bad trip; but I have also had mistaken forecasts which were wrong in my favor so that when I expected some bad weather, the trip was made in sunshine all the way. One never-to-be-forgotten night I had such a tailwind that Shannon could not believe that I was not some sort of jet. It took me only 1 hour and 40 minutes to go 400 miles in an airplane which cruised at 170 knots.

*   *   *

The Pacific Ocean can also spring some surprises on the unwary pilot. Looking at Figure 8-2, we can see that there is a 2000-mile distance from the last weather station in Hawaii to the coast of the mainland, and even West of Hawaii the island reporting points are several hundred miles away from each other. This gives Mother Nature a chance to upset any forecast both in time and in type of weather as well as wind direction and velocity. Fortunately, because of the vast distance from the Asian continent to the North American con-

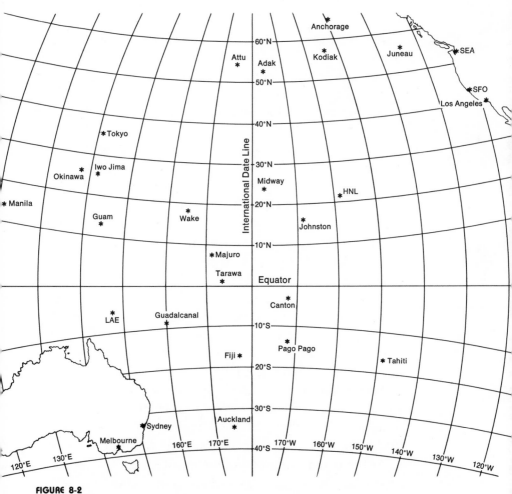

FIGURE 8-2
Pacific Ocean.

tinent in the latitudes below 40° North, the weather systems coming from Asia are somewhat tempered and the air somewhat homogenized by the time it reaches the midpoint of the ocean. Therefore, for most of the year the Central and Eastern Pacific can count on mild weather and light winds.

In the winter the Air Masses coming from Siberia are very strong and very cold. They push much further South and pick up a great deal of moisture as they move over the warmer water until they arrive at the West Coast of North America. Here they deposit that moisture in large quantities of rain or snow, having provided some very unpleasant flying weather over the normally good-weather portions of the Pacific. At this time of year a Westbound flight must sometimes wait many days for the strong headwind to diminish before the 2100-nautical-mile leg from San Francisco to Honolulu or the 2100-mile leg from there to Wake is possible.

Typhoons are spawned primarily in the Western Pacific between July and November and are the same tropical cyclone that we call hurricanes when they occur in the Atlantic or Caribbean. They are equally destructive, and their path, like that of hurricanes, is difficult to predict without hunter airplanes and satellite pictures. Occasionally typhoons develop at other times of the year than the expected July to November.

$$* \qquad * \qquad *$$

South of the equator weather patterns are reversed, and if we are flying to Australia, New Zealand, or the islands of the South Pacific, we need to remember that down there the circulation around a High is *counterclockwise* and that around a Low is *clockwise*. The Trade Winds are from the Southeast, whereas in the Northern Hemisphere the Trade Winds are from the Northeast. This is easy to remember because both Trade Winds blow slightly toward the equator.

At the equator is a belt of what sailors call the *doldrums*, where the pressure is lower than normal, the only wind is random breezes, and the air is hot enough and moist enough to spawn thunderstorms. This area contains the Intertropical Front, which is essentially an East-West line of thunderstorms. These thunderstorms seem to be most violent along the North coast of South America. Here and along the Gulf of Guinea in Africa, there is a diurnal as well as a seasonal movement. In the daytime thunderstorms intensify over the land because it is hotter, and at night move slightly offshore as the land cools slightly. In the Pacific, where there is no significant land mass until we come to New Guinea, the only movement is seasonal—North in our summer and South in our winter. There are many more days when it is possible to fly through this area without encountering thunderstorms than days when we do encounter them, but one must be prepared.

Atlantic or Pacific, I am very cautious about leaving for a night crossing if there is a possibility of bad weather out there; I would rather see what I am getting into. Any ferry pilot can tell some interesting stories of what happened when the forecast was wrong, and these stories are more frequent than they once were.

$$* \qquad * \qquad *$$

In view of these facts let us review some of what we learned about weather when we were studying for our licenses:

1. Standard sea-level atmosphere has a pressure of 1013.2 millibars, or 29.92 inches of mercury, at a temperature of 15°C, or 59°F.

2. Because of the rotation of the earth on its axis and its path around the sun, there are hotter than standard and colder than standard areas, as well as areas of higher than standard pressure and lower than standard pressure; and there is the Coriolis force.

3. These conditions interact to cause Air Masses of different characteristics as well as semipermanent areas of high and low pressures.

4. The movement of these Air Masses and the waxing and waning of the semipermanent pressure areas are what cause the changes in our weather.

5. The dividing line between Air Masses we call *Fronts*. Fronts have the characteristics of their parent Air Mass, but they can be modified by the terrain over which they are moving.

There are several very good meteorology textbooks which go into considerable detail on these points. Our concern is how these weather patterns will affect us in planning a flight over an ocean and help us to ask intelligent questions of the forecaster before we make our decision to go or to wait for better conditions.

*   *   *

Figure 8-3 shows a generalized pattern of pressure distribution over the world's oceans. There is a belt of lower pressure at the equator; between 20 and 40 degrees North and South of the equator is a belt of high pressure, and then again areas of low pressure. In the far Southern Hemisphere, because there are no land masses to affect the circulation, the pressure diminishes evenly toward the Pole. In the Northern Hemisphere, where there are large land masses to affect the circulation, we have the Greenland-Iceland Low in the Atlantic and the Aleutian Low in the Pacific; also what are called the Azores High and Bermuda High in the Atlantic and the Hawaiian High in the Pacific.

In real life of course, the picture is not so neat, but the *tendency* is there. As pilots we are concerned with these pressure areas because of their effect on our flight planning. Both the Aleutian Low and the Greenland-Iceland Low are very vigorous in winter and tend to push more to the South with strong winds and bad weather. On the Atlantic, unless the Low pushes too far South, this will almost guarantee a fine tailwind across to Shannon; if the Low has moved far enough South to spoil the Shannon route, we can expect at least some tailwind to Santa Maria in the Azores.

In the Pacific when the Aleutian Low pushes South and tightens up the pressure gradient between it and the Hawaiian High, we will also have a strong West wind and must plan to sit in the San Francisco area possibly for days until the pressure gradient flattens out and the headwind to Hawaii diminishes enough to accommodate our fuel reserve.

In our summer, when the sun is North of the equator, its more direct rays heat the land areas so that the water is now cooler and the Greenland-Iceland Low in the Atlantic and the Aleutian Low in the Pacific will fill slightly; also the

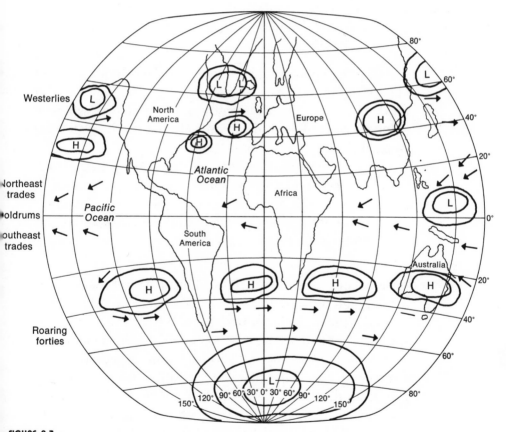

FIGURE 8-3
Pressure distribution over the oceans.

Azores High and the Hawaiian High subside slightly. Now the pressure gradient is shallow and the winds correspondingly diminish; also the weather systems moderate.

The Northern route through Greenland and Iceland now has mostly good weather although we must be cautious about fog in the Narssarssuaq fjord when the wind is Southwest. Also the wind will be light so even if it is not a tailwind it will not do too much damage to our fuel reserve. Another good feature about this route in summer is having practically 24 hours of daylight.

The Shannon route will of course not have much of a tailwind and may even have a crosswind or a slight headwind. The Azores route also will have little help from wind and should be watched for wandering tropical storms.

*   *   *

In the Pacific we will have little or no delay trying to get to Hawaii or points West, because the Aleutian Low has also filled somewhat and stays pretty much up North where it belongs. West of Hawaii we must also be on the watch for tropical storms or typhoons.

This is winter South of the equator, so we can expect stronger winds and more weather over the land masses of Australia and New Zealand; just as in their summer there is the big rain of the tropical regions and the fair weather and light winds of the temperate regions.

*   *   *

Since air is a fluid, it tends to flow downhill, or from an area of high pressure to an area of low pressure. This is particularly true in the lower portions of the atmosphere. From the surface to 10,000 feet, or 700 millibars, this tendency is even more pronounced. Thus we can expect that the Greenland Low will attract any weather systems moving East from the North American Continent; the Azores High will also feed this tendency by obstructing the Easterly movement of the Southern end of any Front. None of these areas are absolutely fixed in position, which makes out-guessing them quite interesting. For us as well as the fore-caster this is an important part of forecasting the wind and weather over the ocean.

Figure 8-4 is a stylized plan of a High and Low Pressure Area in the Northern Hemisphere, indicating the general wind flow pattern. It shows where you must be in relation to the center to have a tailwind and where will be the cross-wind and the headwind. In the Southern Hemisphere these are reversed, of course.

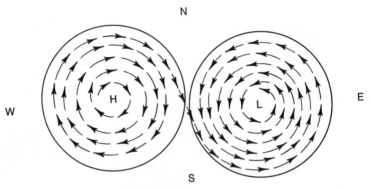

FIGURE 8-4
Plan of a High and Low Pressure Area in the Northern Hemisphere.

Figure 8-5 is an imaginary cross section of the same pressure areas. If we consider that Isobars (which are lines of equal pressure) serve the function of contour lines on a

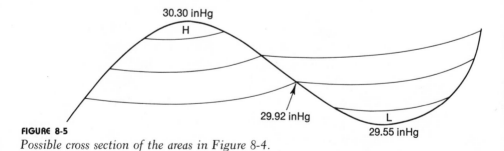

FIGURE 8-5
Possible cross section of the areas in Figure 8-4.

terrain chart, we see that the High (mountain) and Low (valley) have a gradual slope, because the Isobars are far apart. Therefore, the wind will be light.

Figure 8-6 has a steeper slope and the Isobars are close together, so we know that the wind will be fairly strong.

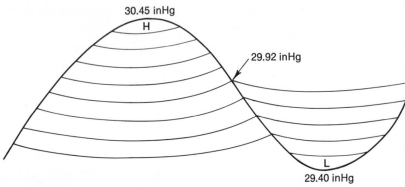

FIGURE 8-6
Another possible cross section of the areas in Figure 8-4, with steeper slopes and Isobars closer together than in Figure 8-5.

When one Air Mass is displacing another, the movement of the Front is influenced not only by the temperature and moisture content of the parent Air Mass but also by the terrain over which it is moving. Flatlands will not impede its progress; mountains will slow it somewhat and will also cause it to leave some of its moisture on the upwind side of the mountain as the air is forced to climb over it. Large bodies of water adjacent to land will tend to slow the Front and will feed more moisture into the air, so the area of clouds and precipitation increases.

In addition to the temperature and pressure differences between two Air Masses, an important determinant of speed and direction of flow is the wind pattern at the 500- and 300-millibar levels. The charts which show these patterns are available at Weather Bureau offices if you ask to see them. If these charts have a strong West-to-East flow aloft, the whole weather system is likely to sweep straight out to sea and even to cross the ocean to Europe without appreciable modification.

If, on the other hand, the upper wind pattern is curved, as it often is, the weather system movement is less decisive; and when it finally gets over the ocean, we can expect to encounter it for a longer distance, although with lower cloud tops and less significant weather in the system.

CHARTS AND SATELLITE PICTURES—ATLANTIC

Figure 8-7 is a 500-millibar chart which extends about halfway across the Atlantic Ocean. We see a Low Pressure Center between Newfoundland and Greenland, with the Isobars curving almost all the way around it. Nowhere on the chart is there a straight flow of these Isobars, and indeed, this Low Center has been wandering around more or less in this area for several days, with nothing to persuade it to move on. A flight made from Iceland to Goose Bay was on top of all clouds and had a tailwind from Iceland to the tip of Greenland, with essentially no wind from there into Goose Bay. The flight was made at 10,000 feet, which is the 700-millibar level (see Figure 8-8).

Figure 8-9 is the chart from the surface up to 500 millibars, and while the Isobars are fairly well in agreement with those on the 500-millibar chart, the indication of High and Low Pressure and the delineation of Fronts running through the middle of the Highs are certainly calculated to confuse the pilot about what he may expect. This is computer work and one of the good reasons for trying to study a satellite picture.

Figure 8-10 is the satellite picture for the same day as the charts. Iceland is around the curve of the earth and not visible, but we can see most of the ocean between Iceland and Greenland at the top of the picture. Looking carefully at it, we notice that the cloud pattern in that area shows a definite wind from the Southeast, which agrees with both the 500-millibar chart and the 700-millibar chart, which latter was drawn by the Iceland forecaster.

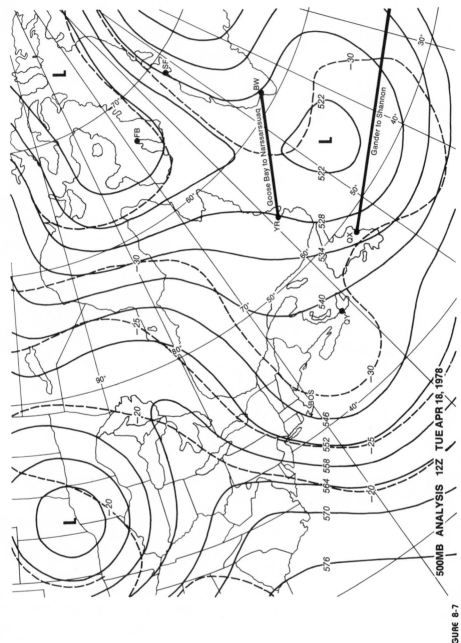

FIGURE 8-7

A 500-millibar chart of part of the North Atlantic.

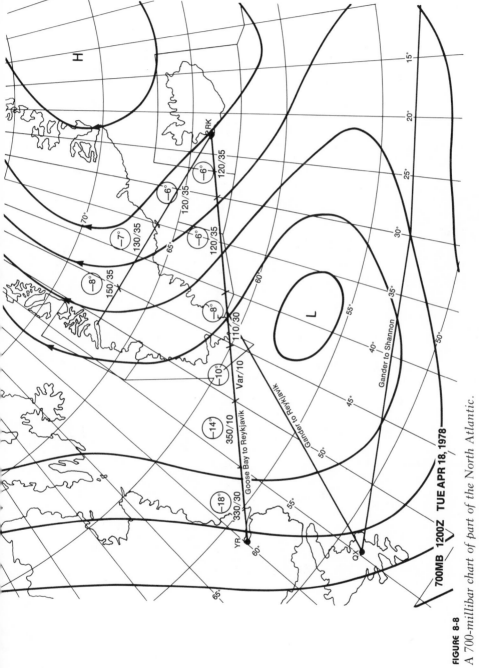

FIGURE 8-8
A 700-millibar chart of part of the North Atlantic.

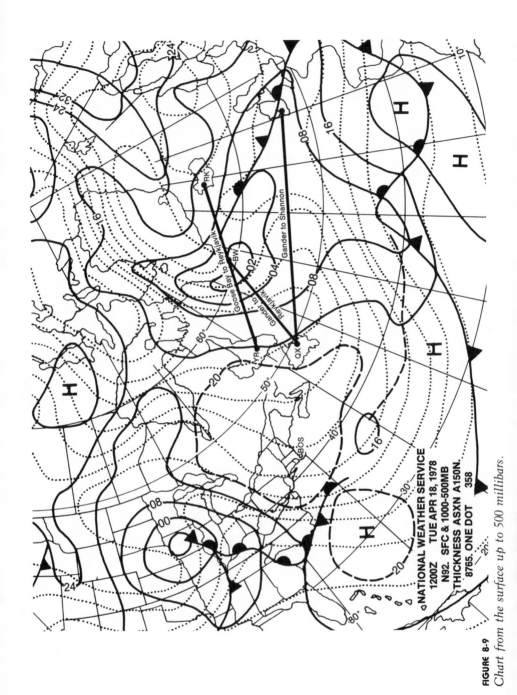

FIGURE 8-9
Chart from the surface up to 500 millibars.

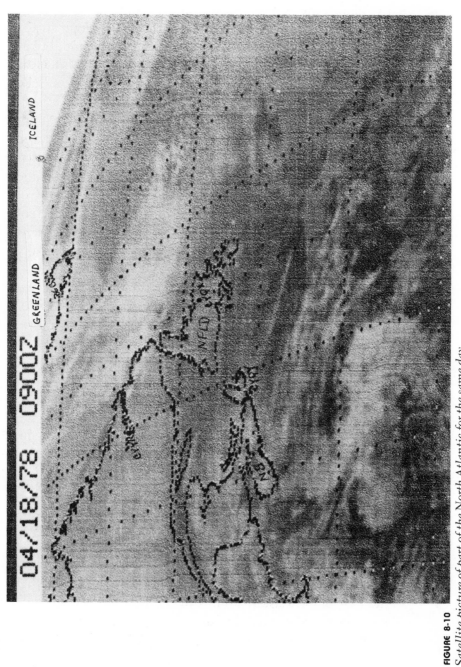

FIGURE 8-10

Satellite picture of part of the North Atlantic for the same day as the charts in Figures 8-7 to 8-9, showing clouds.

Although the picture is not the best, it does indicate that the clouds are in the lower level and should be topped at 10,000 feet, as proved to be the case. It is difficult to tell what kind of weather there is in southern Greenland, but as we move West into the Davis Strait, the wind shows a clear pattern from the North down at least to the Straits of Belle Isle between Labrador and Newfoundland.

To me, it seems that there is another Low Center South of Nova Scotia with a fairly large area of cloud coverage and another Southeast flow around the northern part of that cloud patch. The 500-millibar chart does not show this, and except for the notation on the Canadian Department of Transport Significant Weather Chart of a TROF (a trough of low pressure), it does not seem to be shown on that chart either. The clouds in that area do not look very high or very dense, but the wind pattern looks quite definite.

This picture is what was actually visible at 0900Z when the satellite passed overhead. The charts are an analysis of what the programmers put into their computers as a forecast of conditions at 1200Z. Figure 8-9 is a combination of what the weather would be at the surface, at 10,000 feet, and at 18,000 feet, which tends to make it confusing and prevents it from agreeing with either the satellite picture or the upper-air charts.

Comparing satellite pictures with the Prog charts and the Terminal forecasts is not only very interesting but can also pay off when we come to the go–no-go decision and in peace of mind after we have made that decision.

When we are flight-planning, it is quite helpful to be able to guess at the tops of the clouds which frequently seem to indicate the altitude where the circulation around the Low Center starts changing toward the overall upper-level pattern. If we are below the level of the cloud tops, we find that the North and East quadrants of the Low Center not only have the worst weather but also the most adverse winds for an Eastbound flight. Figures 8-7 and 8-8 indicate that we would have a strong headwind if we were Eastbound from Greenland to Iceland. The upper wind from Goose Bay to

Narssarssuaq, Greenland, although it starts out as a strong North wind, becomes what the Met Office calls "Variable," which means that it could be from the East—or from the West; there is no ship to report these days. However, over Southern Greenland we can assume that the weather on the West coast and at Narssarssuaq will be good, while the weather on the East coast probably will be poor. The West coast in its southern portion has a wind off the icecap, while the East-coast wind is from the sea; it moves upslope onto the icecap and deposits its moisture in the form of low clouds and rain, fog, or snow.

TAFORS (TERMINAL AREA FORECASTS)

Once we leave the United States, we no longer ask for Terminals; in other countries they are referred to as TAFORS or more usually TAFS, and the code used is an international one with a different sequence than we are used to. This code and sequence are also used in the actual weather report. The sky, instead of being divided into tenths as we do, is divided into eighths, which are called *octares*; it is still reported in feet. Visibility is reported in kilometers and meters, rather than our miles and fractions. Since aviation usage is exclusively nautical miles, it will be easier to think only of them when you are mentally converting kilometers and meters into familiar distances. Since 1 kilometer equals 0.54 nautical mile, I just divide the reported kilometers by 2 for a useful visibility estimate. Accurately, 6 kilometers times 0.54 = 3.24 nautical miles, but 6 kilometers divided by 2 = 3 nautical miles, which is close enough.

When the visibility is reported in meters, it can sound quite scary if we have not trained our mind to translate. On a very early trip I requested the weather at my destination and was told that the visibility was 1400 meters with mist. My mind said, "That's ¼ mile and fog." Going into a strange airport at 0400 in the dark under such conditions was not for me, so I went elsewhere and wasted several hours. Discussing it with the local Met Office, I realized what had happened, and ever after I *heard* meters when it was said and automatically multiplied by 3. Since 1400 meters is 4550 feet, it is ³/₄ mile, and mist is much lighter than fog, so the approach would not have been difficult. To be very accurate 1 meter equals 3.28 feet, but when one is in the air and preparing for an approach with all the other things to think about, a quick "times 3" is good enough.

Temperatures are always given in Celsius (formerly called centigrade), and altimeter settings are given in millibars. Outside North America they are not called altimeter settings but QNH, which is the international code for sea-level barometric pressure and thus is the same as altimeter setting. You may be asked at some airports if you would like the QFE. This is the barometric pressure at field elevation. If you use it, your altimeter will read 0 feet on landing.

The types of clouds are also given both in the TAF and the current sequence report. This has the advantage of telling you whether the air is stable or unstable and so whether to expect turbulence or smooth air for your approach and landing.

If you are in the Met Office and reading either the TAFOR or the current weather report, it helps to be able to interpret the code at least somewhat in case the forecaster/briefer does not speak English, which can happen. Here follows the code and its order of presentation.

*   *   *

First is the four-letter station identifier (see Appendix B or the Radio Facility Chart Supplement). This is followed by the range of valid times in GMT, or Zulu. For the TAFOR these are the beginning and end of the period, and for the current weather it is the time of observation (four digits using the 24-hour clock).

Next is the wind usually five digits. The first three digits are *true* direction, and the last two digits are the velocity; if it is gusty, the highest value of gust is indicated; for example, 24015/25 indicates 240°, speed 15 knots, with gusts to 25 knots. The code VRB indicates a variable wind and 00000 indicates no wind, or calm.

Visibility is given in meters in four digit numbers as: 0000, 0400, 0800, 2000, up to 9999, which means more than 10 kilometers, or more than 5 nautical miles.

Obstructions to visibility are two digits followed by two letters with the same meaning.

With numbers from

10–49: the obstructing particles are very small as mist, fog, haze, etc.

50–59: the particles are visible as light rain.

60–69: the rain is moderate.

70–79: the particles are snow.

80–89: the precipitation is showery in type, either rain or snow.

90–99: the precipitation is heavy, like thunderstorms or hail.

The two letters added after the above numbers have the following meanings:

BR	mist	TS	thunderstorm
FG	fog	FU	smoke
DR	drizzle	HZ	haze, dust
RA	rain	SA	sandstorm
SN	snow	PE	ice pellets
GR	hail		

Then there are modifiers:

MI	shallow
XX	heavy or severe
BC	patches
SH	showers
BL	blowing
FZ	freezing
SQ	squall

If you see 65FZ, freezing rain, or 98TS-GR, heavy thunderstorm with hail, you will of course be prepared to go elsewhere.

After the visibility and its obstructions come the clouds in six characters, the first (in figures from 1 to 8) being the amount of sky cover and the next (two letters) for the type of cloud:

ST	stratus	CU	cumulus
SC	stratocumulus	CB	cumulonimbus
NS	nimbostratus	CI	cirrus
AC	altocumulus	CS	cirrostratus
AS	altostratus		

The last three digits are the height in feet above the aerodrome. Indefinite ceiling is indicated by 9//, and approximate height. 9//002 is on the ground.

The TAFOR may also have modifiers:

TEMPO   temporarily during the period

PROB *nn*%   probability of *nn* percent during the period

INTER   intermittently during the period

GRADU   followed by four-digit time means that gradually the weather will change beginning at that time (times are always Zulu)

With this information we can read the TAFORS on the same morning as the weather charts of Figures 8-7 and 8-8:

BIRK	0606	14010	9999	3ST010	8SC025	
	TEMPO	4800	50DZ	10BR	8ST010	
	GRADU	1821	14015/20	4800	58RA	10BR
	3ST004	8NS007				
	TEMPO	0800	59RA	45FG	9//002	

In English, the forecast period is from 0600Z today until 0600Z tomorrow and starts with wind from 140° at 10 knots, visibility more than 10 kilometers (about 5 nautical miles) three-eighths stratus at 1000 feet, eight-eighths stratocumulus at 2500 feet (an eighth is an octare).

The overall weather *might* be like that, *but*

TEMPO   Temporarily the visibility will be 4800 meters (2.5 nautical miles) with light drizzle and light mist, overcast stratus at 1000 feet.

GRADU   Gradually, from 1800Z to 2100Z, the wind will increase to 140° at 15 knots with gusts to 20 knots, visibility 4800 meters (2.5 nautical miles) with heavier rain and light mist, scattered stratus at 400 feet and overcast nimbostratus at 700 feet, but:

TEMPO   Visibility will be 800 meters (approximately ¹/₂ nautical mile) with moderate rain and heavy fog and the ceiling becoming indefinite at 200 feet.

Although the weather at Reykjavik is fairly good this morning, it is expected to deteriorate through the day and more rapidly after dark.

```
BGSF    0606    VRB05    9999    5AC080    7CI180
        TEMPO   0618     24006   1600      71SN    9//010
```

In English, the overall weather between 0600Z today and 0600Z tomorrow: wind is variable at 5 knots, visibility more than 10 kilometers (5 nautical miles); clouds five-eighths altocumulus at 8000 feet, seven-eighths cirrus at 18,000 feet, but:

TEMPO   Temporarily between 0600Z and 1800Z the wind will be 240° at 6 knots, the visibility will go down to 1600 meters (⅞ nautical mile) in snow, and the ceiling will be indefinite around 1000 feet, because of the snow.

So Sondrestrom is expecting changeable weather for most of the day.

```
CYYR    0606    24005    CAVOK
```

In English, from 0600Z today until 0600Z tomorrow the weather at Goose Bay will be very good, with the wind from 240° at 5 knots and visibility more than 10 kilometers (5 nautical miles) and any clouds above 5000 feet.

Tables 8-1 to 8-5 are conversion tables for temperatures, pressures, and distances.

TABLE 8-1   Conversion of millibars to inches

	0	1	2	3	4	5	6	7	8	9
mb	Inches									
940	27.76	27.79	27.82	27.83	27.88	27.91	27.94	27.96	27.99	28.02
950	28.05	28.08	28.11	28.14	28.17	28.20	28.23	28.26	28.29	28.32
960	28.35	28.38	28.41	28.44	28.47	28.50	28.53	28.56	28.58	28.61
970	28.64	28.67	28.70	28.73	28.76	28.79	28.82	28.85	28.88	28.91
980	28.94	28.97	29.00	29.02	29.06	29.09	29.12	29.15	29.18	29.20
990	29.23	29.26	29.29	29.32	29.35	29.38	29.41	29.44	29.47	29.50
1000	29.53	29.56	29.59	29.62	29.65	29.68	29.71	29.74	29.77	29.80
1010	29.83	29.85	29.88	29.91	29.94	29.97	30.00	30.03	30.06	30.09
1020	30.12	30.15	30.18	30.21	30.24	30.27	30.30	30.33	30.36	30.39
1030	30.42	30.45	30.47	30.50	30.53	30.56	30.59	30.62	30.65	30.68
1040	30.71	30.74	30.77	30.80	30.83	30.86	30.89	30.92	30.95	30.98
1050	31.01	31.04	31.07	31.09	31.12	31.15	31.18	31.21	31.24	31.27

TABLE 8-2   Temperature conversion

°C	°F	°C	°F	°C	°F	°C	°F	°C	°F	°C	°F	°C	°F
−40	−40.0	−27	−16.6	−14	6.8	−1	30.2	12	53.6	25	77.0	38	100.4
−39	−38.2	−26	−14.8	−13	8.6	0	32.0	13	55.4	26	78.8	39	102.2
−38	−36.4	−25	−13.0	−12	10.4	1	33.8	14	57.2	27	80.6	40	104.0
−37	−34.6	−24	−11.2	−11	12.2	2	35.6	15	59.0	28	82.4	41	105.8
−36	−32.8	−23	−9.4	−10	14.0	3	37.4	16	60.8	29	84.2	42	107.6
−35	−31.0	−22	−7.6	−9	15.8	4	39.2	17	62.6	30	86.0	43	109.4
−34	−29.2	−21	−5.8	−8	17.6	5	41.0	18	64.4	31	87.8	44	111.2
−33	−27.4	−20	−4.0	−7	19.4	6	42.8	19	66.2	32	89.6	45	113.0
−32	−25.6	−19	−2.2	−6	21.2	7	44.6	20	68.0	33	91.4	46	114.8
−31	−23.8	−18	−0.4	−5	23.0	8	46.4	21	69.8	34	93.2	47	116.6
−30	−22.0	−17	1.4	−4	24.8	9	48.2	22	71.6	35	95.0	48	118.4
−29	−20.2	−16	3.2	−3	26.6	10	50.0	23	73.4	36	96.8	49	120.2
−28	−18.4	−15	5.0	−2	28.4	11	51.8	24	75.2	37	98.6	50	122.0

TABLE 8-3   Conversion of Meters to Nautical Miles

Meters	Nautical miles	Meters	Nautical miles
100	0.054	5,000	2.700
500	0.270	6,000	3.240
1000	0.540	7,000	3.780
2000	1.080	8,000	4.320
3000	1.620	9,000	4.860
4000	2.160	10,000	5.399

TABLE 8-4   Conversion of Meters to Feet and Feet to Meters

Meters	Feet or meters	Feet	Meters	Feet or meters	Feet
0.305	1	3.281	18.290	60	196.852
0.610	2	6.562	21.340	70	229.660
0.914	3	9.842	24.380	80	262.469
1.219	4	13.123	27.430	90	295.278
1.524	5	16.404	30.480	100	328.027
1.829	6	19.685	60.960	200	656.1
2.134	7	22.966	91.440	300	984.3
2.438	8	26.247	121.920	400	1,312.3
2.743	9	29.528	152.400	500	1,640.4
3.048	10	32.809	304.800	1000	3,280.9
6.096	20	65.617	609.600	2000	6,561.7
9.144	30	98.426	914.400	3000	9,842.6
12.192	40	131.234	1219.200	4000	13,123.5
15.240	50	164.043	1524.000	5000	16,404.3

TABLE 8-5   Conversion of Nautical Miles to Kilometers and Statute Miles

Kilometers	Nautical miles	Statute miles	Kilometers	Nautical miles	Statute miles
0.185	0.1	0.115	37.06	20	23.03
0.371	0.2	0.230	55.60	30	34.55
0.556	0.3	0.346	74.13	40	46.06
0.741	0.4	0.461	92.66	50	57.58
0.927	0.5	0.576	111.19	60	69.10
1.112	0.6	0.691	129.72	70	80.61
1.297	0.7	0.806	148.26	80	92.13
1.483	0.8	0.921	166.79	90	103.64
1.668	0.9	1.036	185.32	100	115.2
1.85	1	1.15	370.74	200	230.3
3.71	2	2.30	555.96	300	345.5
5.56	3	3.46	741.28	400	460.6
7.41	4	4.61	926.60	500	575.8
9.27	5	5.76	1111.92	600	691.0
11.12	6	6.91	1297.24	700	806.1
12.97	7	8.06	1482.56	800	921.3
14.83	8	9.21	1667.88	900	1036.4
16.68	9	10.36	1853.2	1000	1151.6
18.53	10	11.52			

CHARTS AND SATELLITE
PICTURES—PACIFIC

Figure 8-11 is the Prog chart of the Eastern Pacific for midnight on 11 June from the surface to 500 millibars. The isobars are quite wide apart, and from the indicated position of the diffuse High it would seem that near the surface there is almost no wind, and what wind there is will be more help than hindrance. Also, no weather is indicated.

The faint dotted lines indicate the Isobars at the 500 millibar level which indicate a headwind out to approximately 145° West with a crosswind from the West-northwest the rest of the way. This is fairly well borne out by the 500 millibar chart of Figure 8-12. The forecast winds for the 700-millibar level are inserted along the track line and also indicate a headwind to 140° West with light and variable winds to 150° West and an East wind from there into Honolulu.

For the first half of the trip, the normally aspirated piston-engine airplane might do better at 6000 feet than at 10,000 (700 millibars), at least from the point of view of wind. This Prog chart does not show any clouds at all, but let's check with the satellite pictures.

The first one (Fig. 8-13) was taken at 2315 GMT, or 45 minutes before the valid time of the two charts; this is 1515 Pacific Daylight Time. There is a classic depiction of the circulation around the Low Pressure Center North of track, and certainly one will expect a headwind as far as 140° West, with very few clouds and those probably mostly high cirrus From 140 to 150° West the wind would seem to be rather a cross headwind and the clouds mostly scattered cumulus. From 150° West to Honolulu, I would expect a light and variable wind, perhaps a bit from the Southwest with broken cumulus clouds and perhaps a few rain showers. Altogether a typical summer trip with about −10 for the wind. This picture was taken with a visual camera.

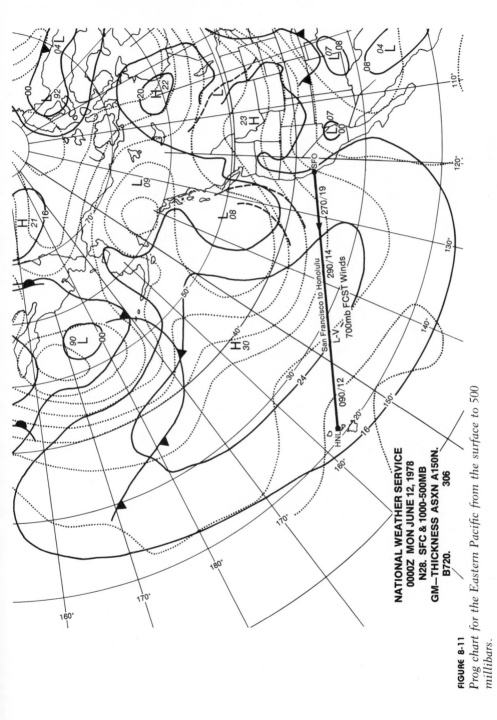

FIGURE 8-11
Prog chart for the Eastern Pacific from the surface to 500 millibars.

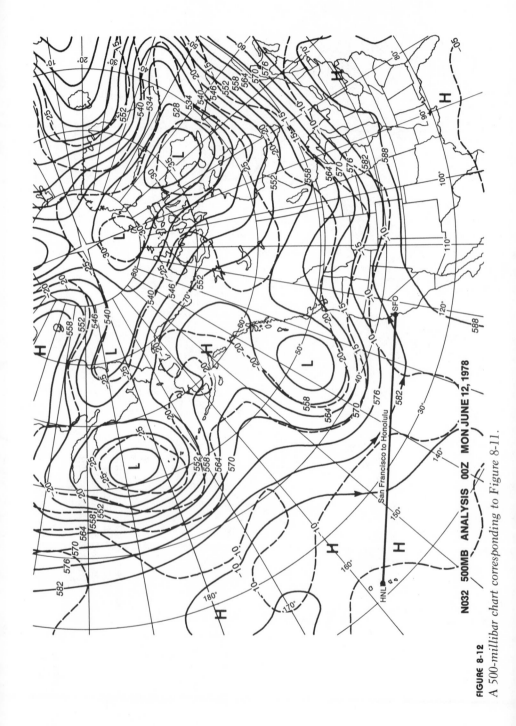

FIGURE 8-12
A 500-millibar chart corresponding to Figure 8-11.

N032 500MB ANALYSIS 00Z MON JUNE 12, 1978

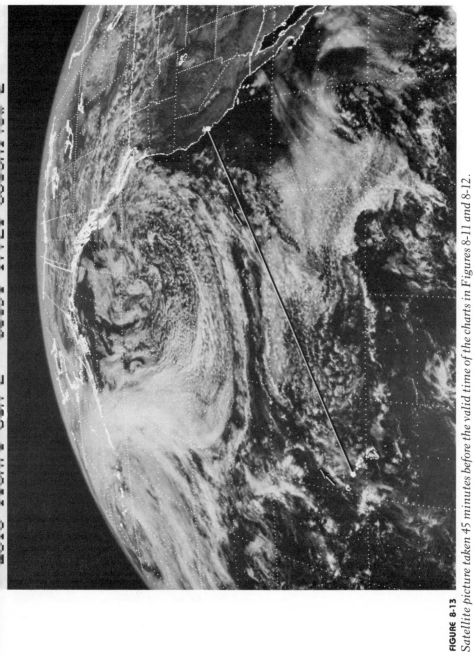

FIGURE 8-13
Satellite picture taken 45 minutes before the valid time of the charts in Figures 8-11 and 8-12.

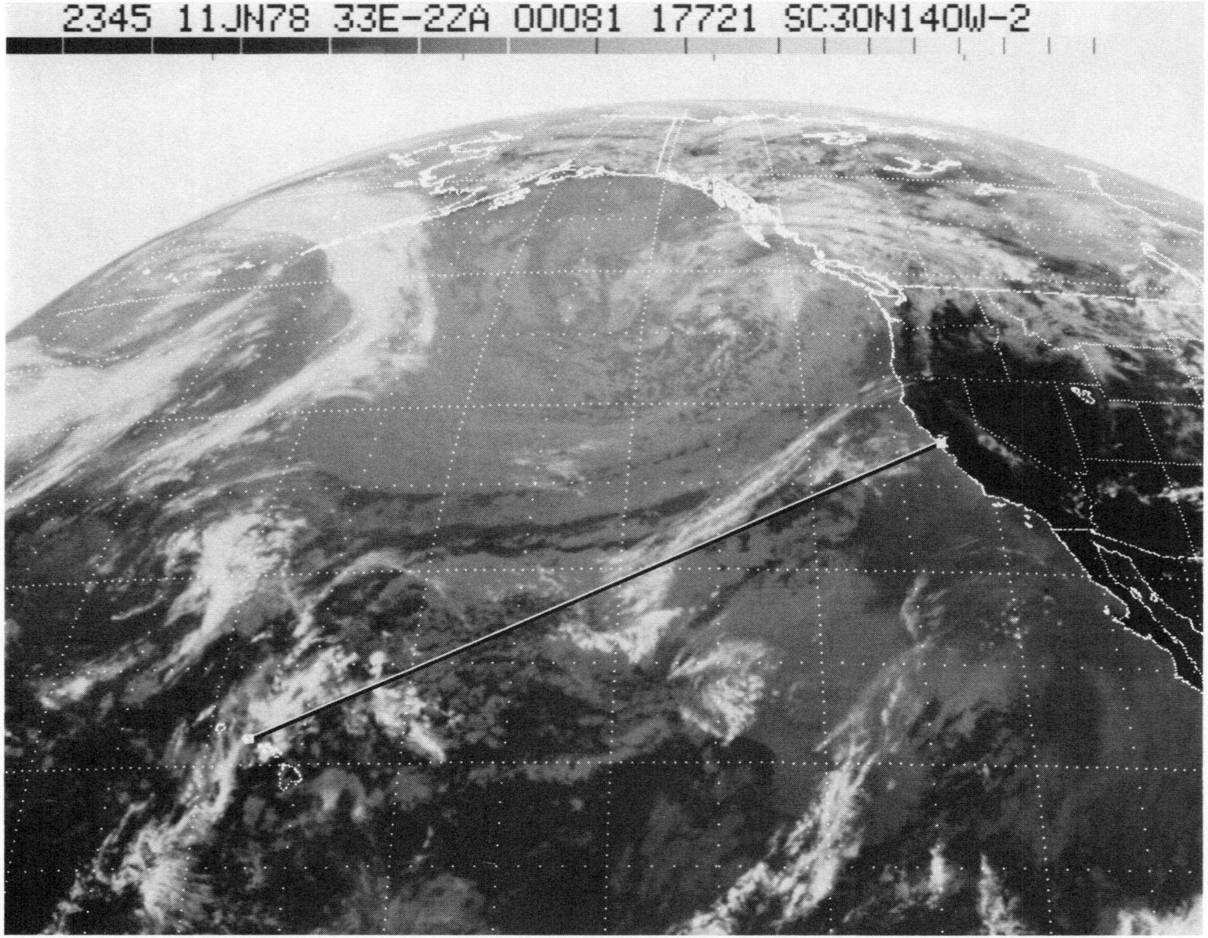

2345 11JN78 33E-22A 00081 17721 SC30N140W-2

FIGURE 8-14

A satellite picture taken with an infrared camera 20 minutes later than Figure 8-12

112

The next satellite picture (Fig. 8-14) was taken 30 minutes later with an infrared camera, and the cloud formations show up somewhat differently. There is a density to the color of the clouds near 140° West and also from 150° West into Honolulu which definitely tells us that there are scattered rain showers in them but nothing to worry about— just typical Pacific summer baby rain showers. It is interesting to note that the Low seems to have only some low clouds near the water and a few high cirrus; all the heavy clouds are to the West, where the surface chart indicated a front.

The Prog chart, the 500-millibar chart, and the satellite pictures all seem to agree that there is another Low coming out of Siberia with a somewhat tighter pressure gradient, so leaving San Francisco in about 6 hours might well give a better wind component in the ridge between the two if one would rather not have −10 for wind component.

WIND/TEMPERATURE

The wind direction and velocity are of importance to a flight from A to B, whether we are over land or water. Over land we frequently pay little attention to them because we can adjust our speed estimates at the next check point or VOR; over the ocean this is not possible, so we look for other means of checking the forecast wind against the actual wind, as any error has the potential of being detrimental to our well-being.

If we are on top of the clouds and those clouds have uneven tops, we can at least make a guess about the wind from watching to see whether the tops are leaning in one direction or another. In tropical or semitropical areas this can also mean that the surface wind is stronger than the wind at our altitude; however in the Northern latitudes we use to cross the Atlantic Ocean the wind is usually stronger at the higher altitudes. Sometimes the difference in velocity between 9000 and 11,000 feet is considerable. I have known times when an airplane slower than mine kept pace with me by going to 11,000 feet while I remained at 9000.

If there are no clouds and the water is visible, one can see the spume blown off the wave crests by the wind, or if the sun is in the right place, one can see wind streaks. However, this only tells the wind direction down there, and it will be somewhat different up where we are, although the change in direction is not as great with altitude over water as it is over land.

Another way to make an educated guess about the wind is to use any change in temperature. We are flying with a forecast wind of West and our OAT is 5°C; if we notice that the OAT has climbed to perhaps 10°C, we can be fairly sure that the wind is now coming from a more Southerly direction. If the OAT drops to 0°C or below, we will not be surprised to find that the wind is now from a Northerly direction. The amount of the change and the speed with which it occurred gives a clue to the degree of the wind shift. This latter method is equally valid whether we are in clear air or in clouds; we know that there is a wind shift on passing a front, for instance.

ICE AND FOG

Ice enroute and fog at destination are the most difficult things to cope with on an ocean flight. Clouds on the North Atlantic any time from September to May should be assumed to have ice in them. If you encounter them too far out to be able to return, there are only two choices: to go up in the hope that there is a warmer layer above or that you can get on top in clear air or to go down in the hope that you can find a layer between clouds or at least some warmer air.

We are of course in clouds when this situation occurs, so the first move is to look carefully above us; if the sun is visible, even though fuzzy, perhaps we can see some signs of blue sky. If we do and the clouds are bright, it is worthwhile to try climbing. We may come out on top at an altitude which we can maintain without oxygen (perhaps we were smart enough to bring oxygen along!), or if the wind is from the South, we may come to a temperature inversion and be in warmer air. This climb must be made before the ice has had a chance to build up on the wings and propeller to rob us of lift and power. Whatever is to be done should be done as early as possible—don't sit there and watch ice build!

If the sun is not able to lighten the clouds and it is gloomy in there, or if the clouds are dense and turbulent, we have no choice but to go down and look for warmer air or at least a layer between the clouds. Between layers, if the temperature is below freezing, any precipitation will be snow, and it will not add to the ice on our airplane. What we already have will stay for quite a long time, as it can only disappear by slow sublimation back into the air. Of course, if we are between layers in above-freezing temperatures, the ice will disappear more quickly.

In stable or smooth air, the temperature normally increases by 2°C for each 1000 feet we descend; if the air is unstable and turbulent, the rules say that the temperature will increase by 3°C for each 1000-foot descent. However, there are many times when we encounter an Isothermal condition, which means that the temperature remains the same for many thousands of feet. I have not yet seen this condition extend all the way to the ocean, but there was one time when I spent some hours at 1200 feet to stay in above-freezing temperatures. More often, I have been able to find an altitude between layers of clouds.

In an airplane with a turbocharged engine which can easily climb to fly on top at 15,000 to 18,000 feet, it is certainly wise to carry oxygen so that the pilot can take advantage of this capability; but *please* do not do it without oxygen. It is *very dangerous*. Pressurized airplanes do have an advantage in these conditions.

$$* \qquad * \qquad *$$

Fog is the nemesis both on the ground at destination and also when flying over the Greenland icecap, where it is impossible to tell the difference between the ice and the fog; more than one airplane now rests there because the pilot could not see which was sky and which was ice and just flew right onto the ice while trying to maintain VFR. Keeping one's eyes on the instruments and absolutely maintaining the enroute altitude is the only solution to this problem.

Fog at the departure airport is a nuisance because of the delay it causes, but no sensible pilot is going to depart from an airport for an ocean flight unless the weather assures that he can come back if necessary for any reason.

The possibility of fog at destination at the estimated time of arrival must be given careful attention at the predeparture briefing. There are, of course, certain symptoms. If the flow of air is from water to land, the wind is light, and the temperature/dew-point spread seems to be closing, one should be suspicious. If the night is clear and calm with small temperature/dew-point spread, fog is 99 percent sure just before and at sunrise. A warm rain over colder air adjacent to the ground can also cause fog, as in a frontal passage with little wind. The temperature/dew-point spread and its tendency (will the sun go down and bring them closer together, or is it early, so that the sun will heat the air and separate them?) are important questions to have answered.

Since all the airports we use for a transocean flight are on or near the seacoast, the relative temperature of land and water will play a part in the likelihood of fog.

MOTHER NATURE AND THE COMPUTER

Meteorology is called a science, but it deals with Nature and there really cannot be any hard-and-fast rules such as two plus two equals four. That statement is always true (except in politics), but Mother Nature does not lend herself to absolute positives. As pilots we know that there are many times when the weather *should* have been one way and *was* another. This is why I suggest studying it as much and often as possible before departing for an ocean flight; it cuts down on the unpleasant surprises.

An example of this is what frequently happens to a supposedly predictable Cold Front as it proceeds Eastward from New England to Nova Scotia and Newfoundland. Until it reached New England, it was oriented in the "normal" Northeast-Southwest direction with its Low Center traveling across southern Canada; the whole system had been moving at the predicted 30 knots. The computer Prog charts indicate that it will continue in this orientation and at this speed until it passes Eastern Canada and goes out to sea, with the center passing over Goose Bay and the front passing the Gander and St. John's area.

Lo and behold! a check of the actual weather through Nova Scotia the next day shows that Yarmouth, Halifax, and Sydney, which are the main reporting stations along the length of the Nova Scotia peninsula, are all covered with low clouds, fog, and either rain or snow (depending on the time of year). The computer says that the front has now passed Gander and St. John's. What has happened? Why has there been no clearing behind it?

What happened is what frequently happens to a Front in this area; perhaps the computer forgot that Nova Scotia, which is aptly called one of the Maritimes, is practically surrounded by water—the Bay of Fundy on the Northwest, the Atlantic on the West, South, and East, and the Gulf of St. Lawrence to the Northeast. It may also be that the Azores High in mid-Atlantic has strengthened and spread a bit to the West, which will block the Eastward movement of the Southern end of this system. In any case, here we are with the Low Center proceeding more or less on course and on time to pass Goose Bay and go out into the Davis Strait toward Greenland, while the Front gets stalled in the Maritimes. Since the orientation has now changed to almost an East-West direction, the possibilities of early clearing are rapidly diminishing. East of a front, the wind is Southeast, and there is plenty of moisture from the ocean to feed the forward Air Mass; behind a front the wind is West or Northwest, and there is also plenty of moisture to feed that Air

Mass from the Bay of Fundy. Now we have the whole area from the West end of Nova Scotia right through to Gander and St. John's on the East coast of Newfoundland under the influence of this increasingly moist air.

Depending on the relative vigor of the two Air Masses, the front may remain stationary, or it may move a bit North as a warm front and then South again as a cold front and keep doing this until some change in the upper-air pattern becomes powerful enough to move it definitely one way or the other. In the United States we are having trouble with it, too, because as the lower end hangs offshore, little secondary low centers form down South and move up along the front. Low pressure always attracts low pressure because, like people, air and water are lazy and take the path of least resistance, which is to follow a trough of lower pressure.

It is an interesting and instructive exercise to watch the hourly sequences of actual weather and compare them with the computer forecasts every 6 hours, and the "amended" forecasts coming from the affected stations about every hour. Forecasters, like the rest of us, are afflicted with the "hope springs eternal" syndrome, and after all, the computer said—.

During this period of stagnation and/or indecision while the Front is losing its push, the tops of the clouds have subsided somewhat, and if there is any place we can go beyond the weather, we can be fairly sure of an on-top flight. Back in the days when single-engine airplanes were not allowed to leave Canada for an ocean flight and my only departing points were Boston, Bangor, or St. Pierre, I would go non-stop from Boston to Shannon and thus overfly all the bad weather in Nova Scotia and Newfoundland. The twins had to stop at Gander for fuel and would be stuck there for several days sometimes. If one of them was destined for the same distributor to whom I was going, it would cause a good bit of comment that the single with a woman pilot got through and the twin with a man didn't. Female chauvinism, I guess, but I enjoyed it.

Should you encounter such a weather picture, rather than go to Gander and get stuck, you might prefer to go to Goose Bay and on to Iceland; however, be sure to check that there is not too strong a headwind.

Another example of Mother Nature not cooperating with the computer can be found in what is called a *closed low*. This is a Low Pressure Center which has formed, usually unexpectedly while nobody was looking, either over land or water. Its cause can be found in a local "hot spot," which hindsight can identify; because the circulation around the center is completely closed off, there is no good way to determine its direction of motion. It has no trough of low pressure to travel along nor any Air Mass to push it in one direction. One can think of a closed low as a balloon drifting on the wind where each vagrant breeze changes its direction.

These closed lows can interfere with our plans quite considerably when they get out over an ocean where there can be no reporting of their position. If they are strong enough to produce hurricanes or typhoons, of course, the Hunter airplanes will go out and track them, so we are warned of their position. However, if the closed low produces only an average type of storm, it will not be tracked and we have no way of knowing where or when we will encounter it; its wind and weather will be unknown quantities in the forecast.

If the Gander Weather Office has seen one of these troublemakers in the last few days, we will do well to proceed with caution in our flight planning over the North Atlantic. If we are crossing the Pacific, we will want to search the weather chart and satellite pictures to ensure that there is not one in those wide areas between reporting points, which could cross our path at an inopportune time and place.

∗   ∗   ∗

Because of pressure gradients which we have discussed, we may have two alternatives to our Great Circle track across an ocean. These alternatives are called *pressure pattern* or *minimal time track*, and *single drift heading*, both discussed in Chapter 9, Navigation.

9

Navigation

N avigation is the science of getting from here to there, whether your vessel is on, above, or under the surface. It is a very old science, having grown and died many times in the course of history and prehistory. My first involvement with navigation, as with the compass, appears to have been in Atlantis over 12,000 years ago. Flying large "ships of the air," I transported a great number of people to Egypt and the Iberian Peninsula before Atlantis disappeared. In this life also, I find navigation a fascinating science.

DEAD RECKONING

This is an old and basic method of navigating although it is far from being the most accurate. The term has no relation to any of the dictionary definitions of the word "dead." According to the *American Practical Navigator*, originally by Nathaniel Bowditch (1773–1838), which is almost a Navigator's bible, the term "dead reckoning" originated from two different methods of estimating position. In one case, the navigator deduced his position from his direction and speed since the last known position, making what allowance he could for wind and current. Naturally the word *deduced* was shortened to *ded* reckoning. In another method a "Dutchman's log" was thrown overboard. This was a buoyant object and was assumed to be *dead* in the water so the speed could be reckoned from it. Obviously, neither of these methods could be considered exact, but they have been in use on the sea for many generations.

In the air we use the direction and velocity of the wind along with our airspeed and course rather than the set of the current, but the position arrived at is still only an estimation. Even though we can supplement the information we obtain from our dead-reckoning wind triangles with radio aids such as ADF, VOR, Loran, Omega, Doppler, VLF, etc., as well as celestial navigation using stars, moon, and sun, the dead-reckoning wind triangle is still an essential part of our ocean-flying procedure. So let us examine the wind triangle and expose its supposed mysteries.

Figure 9-1 is a part of an Aircraft Position Chart 3071, showing the area between Labrador and Greenland. We wish to go from Goose Bay in Labrador to Narssarssuaq in Greenland (called Bluie West 1 during World War II).

The track we draw goes from Goose Bay to the island of Simiutak, lying at the mouth of the fjord, the end of which hides Narssarssuaq. When we measure the angle between *True* North (remember the chart is oriented to *True* North) and our track, we find that at 60° West it measured 041°; at the next meridian, or 55° West, it measures 045°, and at 50° West the measurement is 048° into Simiutak.

In Chapter 7, The Charts, we agreed that on a Lambert Conformal Conic chart a Great Circle track crosses each meridian at a different angle because the round shape of the earth causes the meridians to converge at the Poles. Here we see that even on a fairly short leg we have a difference of 7° in the track from beginning to end.

Since the upper winds are always given with reference to *True* North, we apply the wind to our track to find out what *True* Heading we must fly to hold that track. Let's assume that the wind for our flight altitude has been forecast as 290°

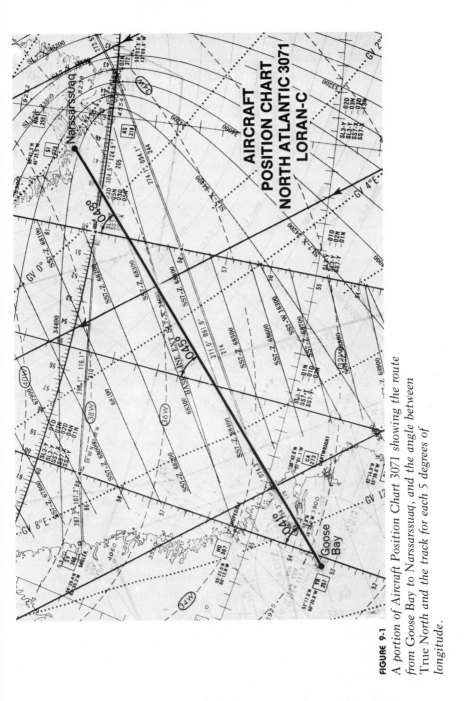

FIGURE 9-1

A portion of Aircraft Position Chart 3071 showing the route from Goose Bay to Narssarssuaq, and the angle between True North and the track for each 5 degrees of longitude.

at 15 knots for Zone 12, which the top of the chart tells us is between 60 and 55° West; in the next Zone, 11, the wind will be from 320° at 25 knots, and in Zone 10 it will be from 340° at 35 knots into Simiutak. From Simiutak up the fjord to Narssarssuaq it will be variable because we will be descending, and the surrounding mountains will have an effect on both direction and velocity. All long-range navigation uses nautical miles for distance measurement and nautical miles per hour, or knots, for speed measurement. Since the wind is also reported in knots, we have apples and apples, and not apples and pears, as would be the case were we using miles per hour for speed.

Our airplane cruises at 150 knots through the air; it will be deflected from the desired track by the direction and speed of the wind, so there are two questions we need to answer:

1. What will be the *True* Heading of the airplane which will compensate for the wind in order to make good our track?

2. How much will the wind increase or decrease our speed over the water (ground) in 1 hour compared with our airspeed?

These wind triangles can be drawn directly on the chart if you wish to be really graphic, but it will add to the clutter and be hard to read. You will probably use a computer, anyway. There are several computers available, and since each has its own instruction book, we will not go into how to use them.

Figure 9-2 shows the wind triangles for Zones 12, 11, and 10 which you need for the trip from Goose Bay to Narssarssuaq. Your computer will give the same answer, but Figure 9-2 illustrates how the computer (or you) arrive at the answers.

1. Start with a reference line which represents a *True* North-South.
2. From a point on this line draw a track line of indefinite length with your plotter. The angles are those we determined on the navigation chart:

a. Zone 12: the angle from *True* North is 041°.

b. Zone 11: the angle from *True* North is 045°.

c. Zone 10: the angle from *True* North is 048°.

3. Now draw a line of indefinite length *from* the direction of the wind.

a. Zone 12: the wind is from 290°, so it will blow the airplane in a direction 110°. On the track side of the reference line draw the wind line *toward* 110°.

b. Zone 11: the wind is from 320°, so draw the line toward 140°.

c. Zone 10: the wind is from 340°, so the line goes toward 160°.

Now that we know the direction in which the wind will blow the airplane, the next step is to determine how far it will blow the airplane in each hour we fly.

4. Using a scale of 1 inch = 50 nautical miles (to keep it all on the paper):

a. Zone 12: measure along the wind line for 15 nautical miles.

b. Zone 11: measure along the wind line for 25 nautical miles.

c. Zone 10: measure along the wind line for 35 nautical miles.

5. All the time the wind is blowing, the airplane is moving through the air at 150 knots of airspeed, so from the end of the 1-hour wind, measure 150 nautical miles to intersect the track line for each zone. This tells us how far along the track we can go in 1 hour with that particular wind.

6. Measuring along the track line from the reference line to the intersection with the airspeed line, we find that:

a. In Zone 12 the wind is a help, and the track line measures 158 knots groundspeed.

b. In Zone 11 we have a crosswind, and the groundspeed suffers; the distance along the track line is 146 knots.

    c. In Zone 10 the wind is more a cross headwind, and our groundspeed suffers still more, at only 136 knots.

7. Going back to answer Question 1, what *True* Heading we need to fly to make good the track, the easiest way is to measure the drift angle.

    a. In Zone 12 the angle where the track line and the heading line join is 07°. This is our drift correction angle, and since the heading line is more northerly than the track line, we must subtract the angle:

Track angle to *True* North =   041°
Drift angle   −07°
True Heading   034°

    b. In Zone 11 the drift correction angle is 10°. Subtracting that from the track of 045°, we have a *True* Heading of 035°.

    c. In Zone 10, the drift correction angle is 13°. By subtracting it from the track of 048° in this zone, we have a *True* Heading of 035°.

You will not always, or even often, come up with the same heading for three or more zones, it just happened in this case.

From a quick check on the distance from Goose Bay to Simiutak, which we measure with dividers along a meridian on the chart, if we keep in mind the fact that 1 nautical mile equals 1 minute of latitude, use the ground speed for each zone, and for the moment ignore the time to climb, we can discover whether we have enough fuel for the trip. Don't forget than after reaching Simiutak, there is still another 45 nautical miles up the fjord to Narssarssuaq. Thus:

Zone	Distance, nmi	Groundspeed, kn	Time
12	270	158	1:43
11	220	146	1:31
10	135	136	1:00
	625		4:14

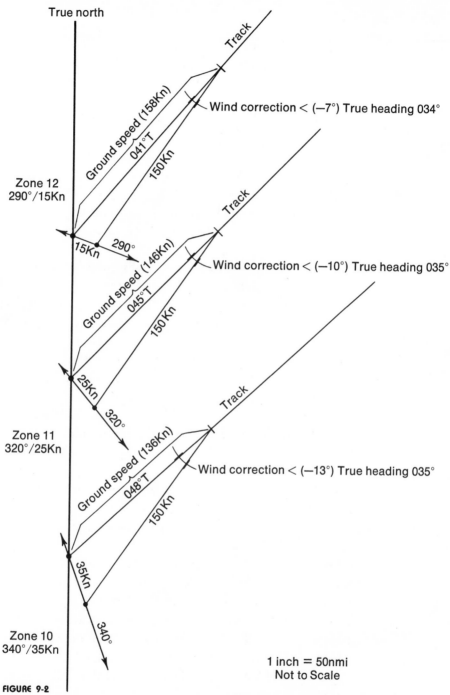

FIGURE 9-2

Wind triangles for the trip from Goose Bay to Narssarssuaq (Zones 12, 11, 10).

Allowing another 20 minutes to go up the fjord and land plus the time and fuel for the climb out of Goose Bay means that very nearly 5 hours' fuel will be gone out of the tanks. Certainly you would not want to start on such a trip without at least 6 hours fuel available, and more would be comforting in case of misplacing oneself or some unexpected change in the weather.

Failing this, one could wait at Goose Bay for a better wind or take the route with shorter legs up through Fort Chimo, Frobisher Bay, Sondrestrom, Kulusuk, and then to Iceland. Discretion is the better part of valor.

$$* \qquad * \qquad *$$

If you have ample fuel and a really good forecast, Figure 9-3 is a sample flight plan, which of course needs to be completed before departure. This is the pilot's working flight plan, and some of it, hopefully, was filled in before leaving home. Reading across the top line: enter the latitude and longitude of each reporting point, the frequencies of any available radio aids, and the zone number; next the distance to the next fix, and the cumulative distance. These columns filled in before leaving home are your basis for determining the feasibility of the trip with your equipment. At the same time the *True* Course and, further over, the Variation can also be filled in.

When you visit the Weather Bureau (in other countries it is called the Met Office), you will learn what the forecast winds are for your route and can then enter that information in the appropriate column.

Then come the wind triangles as we have just done them, for each zone, after which enter the *True* Heading and groundspeed in their columns, not forgetting to allow for climbing time to the first reporting point. Having the *True* Heading, you will *add* the Westerly Variation and enter the Magnetic Heading in its column. The importance of correct application of Variation is clearly illustrated here where the variations are so great; applying 36 and 37° the wrong way will send you up toward the Noth Pole!

SACCHI AIR FERRY ENTERPRISES - OCEANIC FLIGHT PLAN

FROM GOOSE BAY (CYYR)
TO NARSSARSSUAQ (BGBW) ETAS

DATE: A/C   GMT off 1115

FIX	zone FREQ	Dist.	zone dist	cum dist	True crse	Wind	True hdg	Var	Mag. Hdg.	OAT	Alt	GS	T.E.	T. ov	Actual T. ov	Actual GS
100NM		12	100			041°	299°/15	034°	32°W	066°			CLIMB 135	:45	1200		
5530N 57W	GANDER FIR	12	80	180	180	041°	"	034°	34°W	068°			158	:31	1231		
5645N 55W		12	90	270	270	041°	"	034°	35°W	069°			158	:34	1305		
59N 50W		11	220	490	490	045°	320°/25	035°	37°W	072°			146	1:30	1435		
60N 4820W	SOND FIR	10	70	560	560	048°	390°/35	035°	37°W	072°			136	:31	1506		
S1	279KH	10	65	135	625	048°	"	035°	37°W	072°			136	:29	1535		
NA	359KH	10	45	180	670	051°	?	051°	38°W	089°			150	:18	1553		
															4:38		

PNR - Time   Distance

ETP   Tot. Dist x GS Back
        GS out + GS Back

ETP - Time   Distance

Distance   Total

	Time	Fuel
Destin.	4:45	6:00
Alternate		
Reserve	1:15	

FIGURE 9-3

The working flight plan for this trip.

ICAO FLIGHT PLAN
OACI PLAN DE VOL

PRIORITY INDICATOR – Indicateur de priorité	ADDRESSEE(S) INDICATOR(S) – Indicateur(s) de destinataire	≪=
FILING TIME – Heure de dépôt	ORIGINATOR INDICATOR – Indicateur d'origine	≪=
SPECIFIC IDENTIFICATION OF ADDRESSEE(S) AND/OR ORIGINATOR – Identification précise du (des) destinataire(s) et/ou de l'expéditeur		

1 DESCRIPTION	6 AIRCRAFT IDENTIFICATION Identification de l'aéronef	8 FLIGHT RULES AND STATUS Règles de vol et caractère spécial du vol
≪=(FPL	= N 1978 W	= I ≪=

9 NUMBER AND TYPE OF AIRCRAFT Nombre d'aéronefs et type	10 EQUIPMENT – Équipement

| = BE 33 | = COM R / NAV R / SSR U ≪= |

13 AERODROME OF DEPARTURE Aérodrome de départ	TIME Heure	FIR BOUNDARIES & ESTIMATED TIMES Limites de FIR et heures prévues
= CYYR (GOOSE BAY)	1115	→ 5530N 57W/1231 – 60N 4820W/1506 ≪=

15 SPEED Vitesse	LEVEL Niveau	ROUTE
= 0150	F090	→ 100NM – 5530N 57W – 5645N 55W 59N 50W – 60N 4820W – SI

≪=

17 AERODROME OF DESTINATION Aérodrome de destination	TIME Heure	ALTERNATE AERODROME(S) Aérodrome(s) de dégagement
= BGBW (NARSSARSSUAQ)	1553	→ BGSF (SONDRESTROM) ≪=

18 OTHER INFORMATION Renseignements divers
=
57W/1231   55W/1305   50W/1435   SI/1535

)≪=

19 SUPPLEMENTARY INFORMATION – Renseignements complémentaires

ENDURANCE Autonomie	PERSONS ON BOARD Personnes à bord	EMERGENCY & SURVIVAL EQUIPMENT Equipement de secours et de survivance
= FUEL/ 6:30	→ POB/ 2	→ RDO(121.5)→ 243 → 500 → 8364 ≪=

EQUIPMENT Equipement	LIFE JACKETS Gilets de sauvetage	FREQUENCY Fréquence
POLAR → DESERT → (MARITIME) → JUNGLE → (JACKETS) → (LIGHT) → FLUORESCEIN		≪=

DINGHIES Canots	COLOUR Couleur Y	NUMBER Nombre 1	TOTAL CAPACITY Capacité totale 2	OTHER EQUIPMENT Equipement divers
DINGHIES → COVER Y			→ RMK/	

NAME OF PILOT-IN-COMMAND Nom du pilote commandant de bord	Signature of Pilot-in-Command or Designated Representative – Signature du pilote commandant de bord ou de son représentant désigné
)≪= JANE JONES	Jane Jones

FIGURE 9-4
The ICAO flight plan for this trip.

The deviation caused by the airplane can be applied while flying, when changing heading from zone to zone. With the groundspeed and distance, the estimated time to each reporting point is figured on the computer and entered in its column. Your ICAO flight plan must be filed with Air Traffic Control using Greenwich Mean Time (Zulu), so decide now how long it will be before you are ready for takeoff; enter that in the space marked "GMT off," and from there add the enroute times. You can then enter an actual clock time for each reporting point. The last two columns are for what really happens, just in case you do not get off at the exact minute you said or your times change enroute. This gives you a basis for re-estimating subsequent times as you go.

Figure 9-4 is a sample ICAO flight plan. I usually file for FL090 Eastbound and FL080 or 100 Westbound. This is on top of most clouds and takes advantage of 700-millibar winds, but it is still safe without oxygen.

RADIO NAVIGATION

Automatic Direction Finder

The ADF as we know it today in its simplicity of operation has evolved over the last 40 years or so from the fact that a radio antenna composed of a coil of wire is directional in its reception of emissions from a transmitting station. The incoming signal strength is at its maximum when the plane of the coil is in line with the station; when the coil is perpendicular to the station, the signal goes through the "hole in the doughnut" and the signal is at minimum. This is called an *aural null*, or more commonly, just *null*. Since it is easier for the ear to detect the difference between no sound and a little sound than it is to decide between a loud sound and a louder sound, the first radio compasses were based on the aural null. The antenna was a coil of wire wrapped around the tail of the airplane, so that in order to find the null, the whole airplane had to be turned in one direction and the other (see Figure 9-5*a*).

Having found the null, the pilot knew the transmitting station was either ahead of or behind the airplane. This ambiguity was unavoidable for many years, so unless you had some other reason for thinking you knew the position of the station in relation to you, it was necessary to find another station to cross check with the first or, in those days, a landmark which you could identify.

When these first loop antennas appeared on the scene, we were delighted, because even in their crudity, they gave more possibilities of locating ourselves than the four-course radio ranges.

The next great step forward was a rotatable loop, which was a large, covered coil of wire mounted on the cabin roof, with an azimuth dial on the ceiling and a pointer to tell in which direction the loop was pointing. Now, instead of turning the whole airplane, we could turn the loop and read on the dial whether the station was ahead (or behind) or off to one side. The ambiguity, of course, was still there (see Figure 9-5*b*).

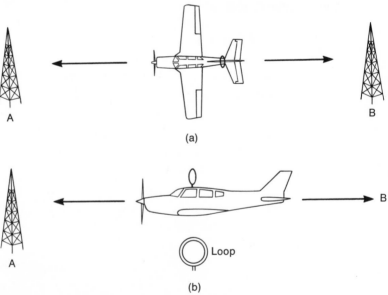

FIGURE 9-5

Finding the station by means of an aural null. (a) *Old method of turning the whole airplane;* (b) *later method, with rotatable loop.*

Improvements came rapidly during the war; and after the war some of them filtered down to general aviation airplanes. One of these was a loop which could be mounted either in the tail cone or in a fairly small housing on the belly of the airplane with a motor to drive it; the other was an additional antenna which gave the sense of whether the station was ahead or behind. This antenna eliminated the old ambiguity and was, of course, called a *sense antenna*.

A few years later the remarkable advances in circuitry, ferrite cores, tiny crossed loops, and other things I don't understand produced the modern ADF, with its little brain which finds the station for us and points to it with what seems to me white magic.

For several years the azimuth dial was fixed in relation to the nose of the airplane. This meant that any bearing was relative to the nose of the airplane, rather than to *True* North, so that in order to plot the bearing on the chart, it had first to be changed to a *True* Bearing.

Figure 9-6 shows how we do this by:

1. Changing the Compass Heading to Magnetic Heading to *True* Heading

$$115° \pm \text{Deviation} = 113° - \text{Variation} = 090° \ True$$

2. Add the *True* Heading of the airplane and the Relative Bearing of station. For station A in Figure 9-6

True Heading	090°
Relative Bearing	+300°
	390°
	−360°
True Bearing of Station	030°

Assuming no wind, turning to 030° *True* will take us to the station. If we want to plot it on the chart, we must use the reciprocal, or 210° *True*. Of course, if we do want to fly to the station, we must add the Variation and the Deviation to get back to a Compass Heading.

FIGURE 9-6

Changing a bearing relative to the nose of the airplane to a
True *Bearing.*

	Station		
	A	B	C
True Heading of A/C	090°	090°	090°
Relative Bearing	300°	045°	210°
	−360°		
True Bearing of station	030°	135°	300°

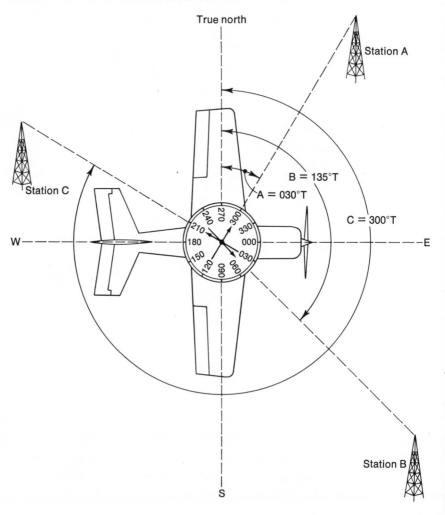

Complaints about the arithmetic involved in this and the possibility of error in changing back and forth finally led to an azimuth dial which is rotatable (Figure 9-7). Now, if the *True* Heading of the airplane is set on the lubber line of the dial, we can read the *True* Bearing directly. The only arithmetic involved is converting Compass Heading to *True* Heading and finding the reciprocal for plotting purposes. Life is much simpler. Never forget though, that to plot on any chart, you must make everything refer to *True* North unless the station has a Magnetic Compass Rose printed on the chart.

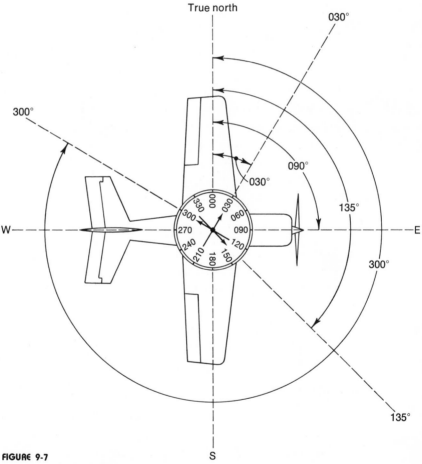

FIGURE 9-7
Reading the True *Bearing directly with a rotatable azimuth dial.*

Since the advent and widespread use both here and abroad of VORs (Very high frequency, Omnidirectional Radio ranges), almost all the old four-course radio ranges over the world have been changed to NDBs (NonDirectional Beacons). These stations send out their emissions in all directions, and we can receive them equally well from any position around the compass. Therefore, our ADF can be used either for homing, when we wish to proceed to the station, or for cross checking when we are proceeding to another station.

Quadrantal Error

The direction-finding loop mounted on an airplane is subject to a *quadrantal error* because the currents induced in the metal structure tend to change the direction of the incoming signals. This error is zero on fore-and-aft bearings if the loop has been installed properly, is minimal on beam bearings, and reaches a maximum on the quadrantal bearings, that is, 45°, 135°, etc. The airplane should be swung on a strong station; with the nose reading zero, take a reading every 45° using the directional gyro (DG) for reference. The readings on this table refer to the nose of the aircraft rather than to Magnetic North.

Night and Twilight Effect

ADF bearings taken at night or at dusk or dawn can be as much as 15 to 20° in error because some of the signal bounces off the Heaviside layer of the sky, and the resultant sky waves come to your receiver at a different angle from the normal ground waves. This leads to confusion in the ADF, and your track may be only a rough approximation of the one you want.

Precipitation Effect

When flying in heavy precipitation, the electric currents generated by the precipitation will deflect the ADF needle from its business, and it will wander and become fairly useless for accurate navigation. Even when the precipitation is light, if there are buildups of cumulonimbus clouds, whether or not they have developed into thunderstorms, the needle has an overpowering urge to point to the buildup as a stronger source of electricity than that which the station is sending out.

Coastal Effect

When one is over water and using a land-based NDB, one must be careful to allow for the coastal effect on the accuracy of the bearing. As the signal crosses a coastline, it becomes bent, as illustrated in Figure 9-8. If your track to the station crosses the coast at a 90° angle, this distortion is minimal, but if the track to the station crosses at a fairly small angle to the coastline, the distortion is sufficient to lead you astray. It is wise to look with a suspicious eye at any bearing which has a small angle between you and the coastline.

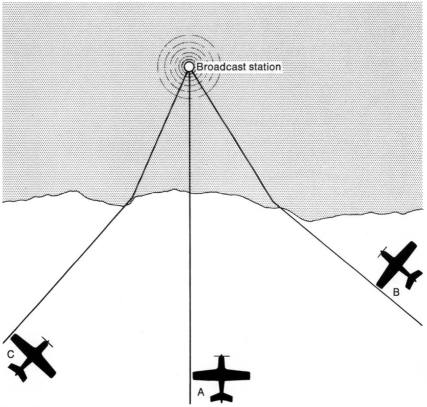

Figure 9-8
The bending effect of a coastline on ADF bearing.

Homing, or Tracking, Inbound

The ADF is not exactly like the VOR in method of tracking to a station, or homing, as it is sometimes called. There is not a definite track displayed on the dial, such as the Left-Right needle of the VOR. Therefore, the pilot must remember that although any kind of crosswind will blow the airplane away from its track, the only indication with an ADF will be that the needle moves from the dead-ahead position to one side or the other. Nothing says to you as loudly as the Course Selector Left-Right needle of the VOR that you are drifting and must change your heading to remain on the selected radial. There is only a measly little change in a needle which is probably wiggling a bit anyway. You must be alert to see this needle change and correct for drift.

Figure 9-9a shows the curved path you will follow if you endeavor to track toward a station with a crosswind by keeping the needle directly on the nose. The stronger the wind, the further from the desired track you will drift, until you end up coming upwind to the station.

If you are supposed to be flying an airway, you will upset Air Traffic Control no end by drifting across another airway which also has traffic on it, possibly at your altitude where there is a danger of collision.

If you are over the ocean and tracking to a shore station from a long distance out, there is the danger of blowing so far off track that you may run short of fuel before finally achieving your destination from downwind.

Figure 9-9b illustrates the method of tracking with an ADF, no matter what the strength of the crosswind.

1. When reception is strong enough to give a good, solid point on the needle, hold the heading for about 10 minutes and watch whether the needle continues to point straight ahead, or whether it moves off to one side or the other, indicating that you have a crosswind.

2. After determining that the wind is from the right, as in this example, if the needle points fairly steadily 15° to the right of the nose, you can assume that the drift is 15° to the left. This means a definite correction to the right to maintain track.

3. Make a turn into the wind (to the right) of 30°. Your *True* Heading was 045°; adding 30°, you are now on a *True* Heading of 075°. Hold that heading until the needle reads 30° to the left of the nose. You are now back on track.

4. To hold the track now that you are on it again, turn to a *True* Heading of 060°, which is 045° plus the 15° of your drift. The needle is now pointing 15° to the left of the nose. If you have a rotatable dial it is pointing to 045°, which is, of course, the track you are trying to make good to the station.

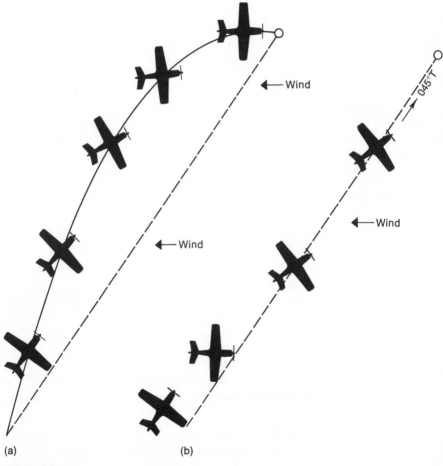

(a)   (b)

FIGURE 9-9
(a) *The curved path a crosswind will cause if the ADF needle is kept directly on the nose;* (b) *the correct method of tracking with an ADF in a crosswind will give a straight line to the station.*

If you have, indeed, arrived at the proper drift correction, you can track all the way in with the ADF needle remaining 15° to the left of the nose, or on track. Essentially, this is what we do with a VOR, except that with the VOR we don't have to figure out the drift angle for ourselves; but in either case, we will crab a bit to remain on track.

Should the needle move off that point to one side or the other, it means that your first drift correction was not quite right, and you will have to go through the above four steps again. There will be some heading which is correct, and you can find it. This will take some practice before it comes easily, but it is worth whatever effort it takes. We have very few NDBs in the United States these days, but there are plenty of commercial broadcasting stations marked on our charts, and we can practice on them whenever we fly.

LORAN

Loran (Long-Range Naviagation) was developed during World War II when crossing the oceans in an airplane became necessary and frequent; it is also used by ships and fishing boats. Loran A, which was the original type, is being phased out and Loran C is what will now be available. Loran C is more accurate for fixing position than Loran A. It uses a different receiver and a slightly different technique; however, the end result, which is to fix our position, is the same. The newer charts have Loran C lines of position (LOPs). Figure 9-10 is a portion of an Aircraft Position Chart 3071 with Loran C stations and LOPs.

Loran is a time-differential method of fixing position. The receiver measures the difference in time of arrival of signals from a Master Station and one or more Slave Stations; this difference is measured in nanoseconds (billionths of a second).

Since there are several Loran C receivers on the market and each varies slightly in method of operation, we will not go into any detail here. Suffice it to say that when you get a line of position from one station, plot it on the chart and

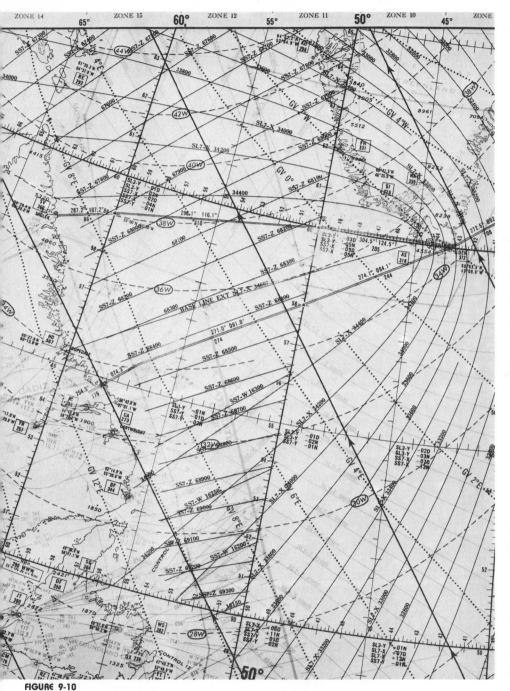

FIGURE 9-10

A portion of Aircraft Position Chart 3071 showing Loran C
stations and their LOPs.

cross it with a line of position from another station, the intersection of the two lines is where you are. With the receiver in the tracking mode, the electronic brain in it will keep constant watch on the track you are actually flying.

Receiver range is between 800 and 1200 nautical miles, depending on the strength of the transmitting station. So far, at least, only the Northern Hemisphere has Loran coverage.

To go around the Northern route to Europe without Loran is safe enough, as the legs are short and there is little time when one is out of ADF range, but to go either the Shannon route or the Santa Maria route, where the legs are very long and the target small, is quite dangerous.

PRESSURE PATTERN FLYING

Pressure pattern techniques are designed to take advantage of the fact that atmospheric pressures are not the same over all the earth; because of this upper wind patterns will vary.

Although the Great Circle course is the shortest *distance* between any two points, it is not necessarily the course which can be flown in the shortest *time*. Pressure patterns cannot offer us a perpetual tailwind, but they do offer us a way of minimizing our flight time by selecting a track which takes advantage of better winds with a slight increase in distance flown. The exact determination of a *minimal time track* is a difficult problem, and in actual practice we achieve only an approximation.

We already know that the wind flows along the contours (or isobars) and that in the Northern Hemisphere the lower pressure will be to the left when the wind is at the observer's back. The speed of the wind is directly proportional to the pressure gradient. This is the geostrophic wind, which is possible because the Coriolis force pulling the moving air to the right of the Isobars counterbalances the pressure gradient which is pulling the moving air to the left of the Isobars toward the area of lower pressure. (This delicate balance of natural forces is another fascinating proof that the universe and our small planet are ruled by a greater Power than we can conceive.)

Figure 9-11 is a chart of the North Atlantic showing the Great Circle course from Gander to Shannon, the contours of the Greenland Low and the Azores High, and a track we can use to minimize our flight time from Gander to Shannon. The Great Circle track will have very little help from the wind as that wind is fairly light and never a direct tailwind. By going from Gander to the 50th parallel at about 45° West and then following that parallel to 25° West before we turn Northeast to Shannon, we can take advantage of the increased pressure gradient, stronger winds, and the almost tailwind for most of the way. This track will be 1760 nautical miles as against 1710 nautical miles for the Great Circle, but we will probably save at least 1/2 hour, so that would be a minimal time track.

Figure 9-12 shows the same area with the Iceland Low and an Azores High which has moved quite far North. Here, the Great Circle track does have some tailwind, but by going up to 55°N at 40°W, flying the 55th parallel East to 15° West before turning Southeast to Shannon, we can once again take advantage of the tighter pressure gradient and stronger tailwind. Again the distance is 1760 nautical miles against 1710, but the time will be less.

The accuracy of this method is only as good as the accuracy of the upper-wind forecast, and there's the rub. A careful comparison of the satellite picture with the upper-wind chart, the digital winds, and the surface chart is essential. Also some searching questions must be asked about *why* the forecast should be acted upon. After all, if the winds are not as forecast, you have gone out of your way for nothing and will waste both time and fuel.

I have used this method several times successfully and a couple of times unsuccessfully. Once I met a pilot at Gander who was going Great Circle to Shannon with an airplane of equivalent speed; I went the 55° North route and beat him by 1 whole hour.

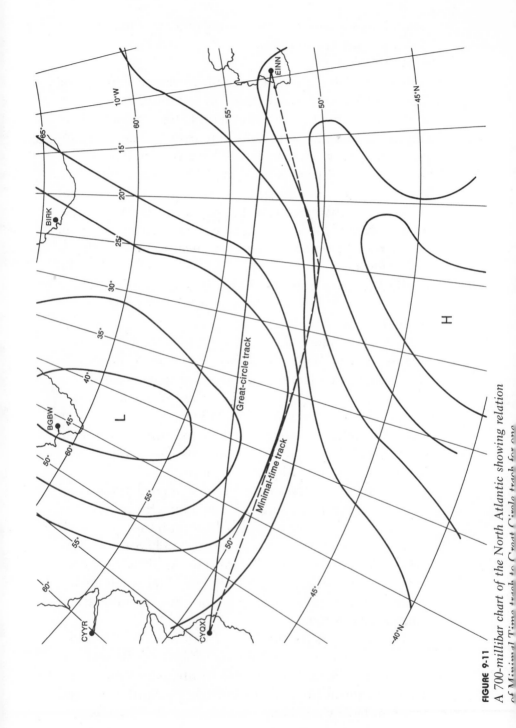

FIGURE 9-11

A 700-millibar chart of the North Atlantic showing relation
of Minimal Time track to Great Circle track for one

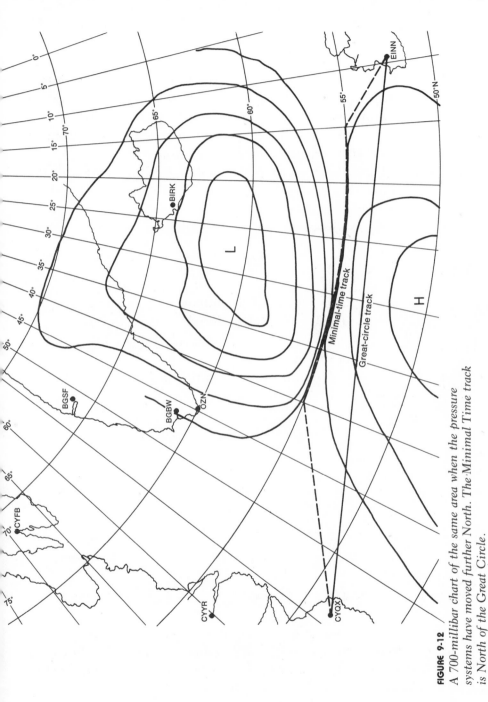

FIGURE 9-12

A 700-millibar chart of the same area when the pressure systems have moved further North. The Minimal Time track is North of the Great Circle.

The other method of using pressure patterns, called *single drift correction*, is far less useful and more chancy. It depends on the difference between the pressure at flight altitude of the departure point and the forecast pressure over destination at time of arrival; you can see the possibilities for error here. The theory is that the opposite drifts between low pressure and high pressure will cancel each other out over the distance traveled. It also requires a radar altimeter for checking against the pressure altimeter.

Figure 9-13 shows a 500-millibar pressure chart with the single drift method illustrated. The 500-millibar contour line over Gander is at 18,000 feet; it is forecast to be 18,600 feet over Shannon at arrival. We have a formula

$$\frac{(D_2 - D_1)K}{\text{TAS}} = Z$$

where D_2 = 500-millibar altitude at destination
D_1 = 500-millibar altitude at departure point
K = factor for latitude (see Table 9-1)
TAS = *true air speed*
Z = drift distance in nautical miles

TABLE 9-1   Values of Latitude

Latitude	K	Latitude	K
22–25°	54	39–43°	33
26–28°	48	44–50°	30
29–31°	44	51–55°	27
32–34°	40	56–62°	25
35–38°	36	63–75°	23

Using the Figure 9-13 and Table 9-1 numbers, we have

$$18,600 - 18,000 = 600 \times 27 = \frac{16,200}{180 \text{ kn}} = 90 \text{ nmi}$$

We will therefore have a drift of 90 nautical miles over the total distance of 1700 nautical miles from Gander. Since we are going from lower to higher pressure, we must correct to the right to make good our track. There are two ways we can do this. As in the illustration, we draw a line 90 nautical miles long to scale upwind at Shannon and connect it with Gander. This line will be our *True* Heading, and the angle between it and the track will be the drift correction angle. We can also work it out on the computer, knowing that $1° = 1$ nautical miles in 60 nautical miles, or algebraically

$$\frac{\text{Drift, nmi}}{\text{Distance}} \; \& \; \frac{\text{drift angle}}{60} \quad \text{or} \quad \frac{\text{Drift, nmi} \times 60}{\text{Distance}} = \text{drift L}$$

$$\frac{90}{1700} \; \& \; \frac{3.18°}{60} \qquad \text{or} \qquad \frac{90 \times 60}{1700} = 3.18°$$

Always when going toward higher pressure the drift angle is added to track angle, and going toward lower pressure the drift angle is subtracted from the track angle.

Because of the uncertainty of the forecast pressures, it will be necessary to monitor the track made good in flight by using the comparison between the pressure altitude and the radar altitude, so that changes in heading can be made as necessary to stay more or less on track.

$$*\qquad *\qquad *$$

Whether we are flying a Great Circle track, a minimal time track, or a single drift pattern, we still must do some navigating to be continuously aware of the track made good and the groundspeed. It is fairly easy to get lost over an ocean, and one needs a lot of luck to find a safe haven when one allows such a situation to develop. There was a pilot heading for Shannon with no navigation equipment who landed on the beach at Porto, Portugal, with 3 gallons left in his tanks. Porto is 700 nautical miles South of Shannon. There was another who crash-landed in the Faroes while heading for Shannon, and that is 550 nautical miles Northeast of Shannon. Several have flown out their fuel and were not heard of again. There is actually no excuse for this, because it is not too expensive to buy or too difficult to use a navigation device.

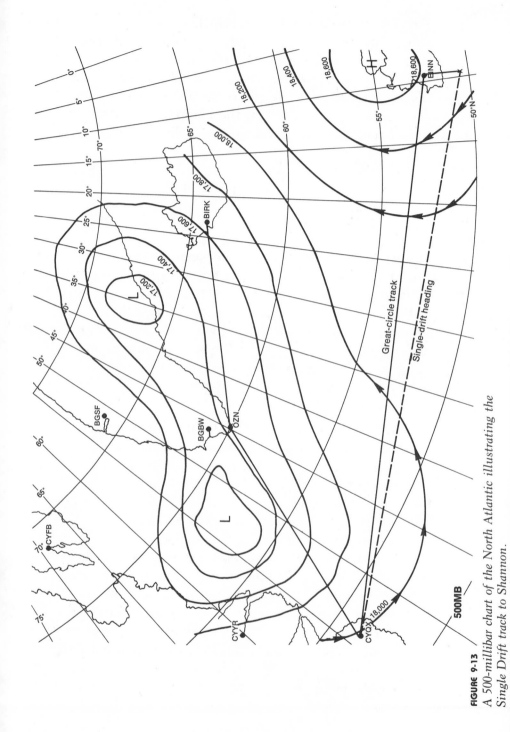

FIGURE 9-13

A 500-millibar chart of the North Atlantic illustrating the Single Drift track to Shannon.

In the lower levels (below 27,500 feet) and for the smaller pocketbooks, Loran C is available and reasonably inexpensive. Above 27,500 feet the ICAO has rules which require dual systems, which can be Inertial, Omega, VLF, Doppler, etc. These are all expensive and heavy, but the airplanes at that altitude or higher are larger and the expense is not as important. Also any airplane above 27,500 feet is competing with the airline aircraft for *Lebenstraum*. There are only a certain number of tracks available. Everybody travels at the same time and wants the same altitude, so navigation must be fairly accurate to maintain a given track.

CELESTIAL NAVIGATION

To make use of stars, moon, and sun for navigational purposes, one needs a bubble sextant, the appropriate charts and tables, and of course, an extremely accurate chronograph set to Greenwich Mean Time. Since all celestial time refers to GMT, any error in the timepiece reflects in an error in the calculated position. There is also a considerably better chance of accuracy if one has an autopilot to fly the airplane while the human pilot struggles to hold the heavenly body in the bubble long enough to read the angle several times for an average. For this reason, as well as the fact that in the lower levels of the atmosphere we frequently have a cloud cover to obscure those heavenly bodies from our sight, celestial navigation is not the most valuable method for us in general aviation airplanes.

CONCLUSIONS

The ability to do the wind triangles for dead reckoning, the ability to use ADF with its drift problems, and the use of Loran for long trips such as to Shannon or Santa Maria from Gander (or across the Pacific) are practical necessities for crossing the watery wastes of any ocean.

An interesting item from the March 1978 issue of *News from Iceland* seems to point up some of what we have been discussing in this chapter.*

One night in late February, when Iceland Air Traffic Controllers became aware of a mysterious plane flying some 75 miles south of Keflavik Airport and heading in the direction of northern Norway, they took immediate steps to establish contact. To everyone's amazement, it was learned that the aircraft, a Boeing 707 cargo transport bound from Bermuda to a point near London, had flown 700 miles off course. The pilot thought he was over Shannon Airport in Ireland when he was passing the southwest corner of Iceland.

That was only the first in a mind-boggling series of events. Once notified of his position the pilot requested permission to head for the intended destination—but after flying a considerable distance, he returned and landed at Keflavik Airport.

What went wrong? The pilot mentioned malfunctioning navigation gear. Icelandic maintenance personnel checked the equipment, which was found to be in perfect working order. The following day, when they wanted to get additional information from the pilot, they discovered that he and the rest of his crew had left for the U.S. on board a commercial jetliner.

Remaining behind were the four owners of the aircraft—all residents of Bermuda. Later the same day, a private jet brought a new crew from Britain, and they took off in the abandoned plane —after confirming that its navigation equipment functioned the way it should.

Iceland air traffic controllers theorized that the real problem was lack of experience in long-distance navigation over water.

My only comment on this is that it is not the first time it has happened, and will not be the last. The best navigation equipment available is of no use, if you don't know how to use it.

---

* Used by permission.

10 Route Characteristics of the North Atlantic

The North Atlantic Ocean offers us four possibilities for crossing by air. We can choose our route after due consideration of:

1. The range of our airplane
2. The extent of our navigating ability
3. The amount of time we have available
4. The scenery in which we are interested
5. The amount of extra equipment we are willing to buy (or try to rent) and learn to use

The time of year will also have an important bearing on consideration of which route to use, although for any route the period between the beginning of June and the middle of September is the best. Then the days are long; in the North there is daylight for most of the 24 hours; we are less likely to find clouds with ice in them; and wind and rain, when encountered, will not be so bone-chilling.

GREENLAND AND ICELAND
ARE INTERESTING

For an airplane with fairly short fuel range, the route will go from the United States border up to Fort Chimo on Ungava Bay in Northern Quebec, from there North to Frobisher Bay in the Northwest Territories of Canada, across the Davis Strait to Sondre Stromfjord in Greenland, across the icecap to Kulusuk on the East coast of Greenland, across the Denmark Strait to Reykjavik in Iceland, from Reykjavik to the Faroe Islands, then South to Stornoway or Glasgow or Prestwick in Scotland.

On this route, the longest leg is 480 nautical miles, from Frobisher to Sondrestrom.

After leaving the United States, the first stop in Canada must be an airport which has Customs facilities. An airport with international traffic is best because if the inspector must come out from town, the charge can be high after hours, just as it is in our own country.

Not very far North of the St. Lawrence River we run out of civilization. The scenery is composed of trees and lakes; it is hard to imagine as many lakes as we see in all shapes and sizes. There are some NDBs and some VORs, but map reading and holding a heading are essential. There are not many airports but plenty of mines and hills (and moose if you are low enough). Places to stay overnight are not plentiful either, so it is wise to check the availability of accommodations before embarking. If you are leaving from the Eastern part of the United States, Sept Îles, on the St. Lawrence about 280 miles Northeast of Quebec and 220 miles Northnortheast of Presque Isle, Maine, is a good stop. The people at the airport are friendly and the overnight accommodations are good.

From Sept Îles to Fort Chimo is 475 nautical miles, and you go over Wabush and Schefferville, both having airports and VORs. Wabush also has instrument approaches if you need them. Fort Chimo lies on the southwest corner of Ungava Bay; it has instrument approaches and Esso fuel, but on Sunday there is a charge for the fuel truck to come out. Don't plan to stay here, as it is only an Eskimo settlement with a few Canadian government employees and no accommodations of any kind. However, it is quite interesting to ride around town and see what there is—it won't take long (Figure 10-1).

FIGURE 10-1
Fort Chimo Eskimo settlement, and its airport in the background, still have snow around the end of May.

From Fort Chimo the airway goes on to Frobisher Bay, 339 miles due North on Baffin Island. It follows the West shore of Ungava Bay past Akpatok Island and then across Hudson Strait and the Meta Incognita Peninsula to Frobisher Bay, at the head of which are the town and airport of Frobisher. Again the scenery is of nature, with only an occasional sign of civilization. Summer is short and comes late, but it is worth seeing.

The airport at Frobisher has only one runway, North-South; on the East side are the buildings; the one with all the available services is the large one at the North end of the ramp (Figure 10-2). Parking in front of it is the best idea, near the Met Office, Flight Service, telephones, and, if you are lucky, the lunchroom. Frobisher also has a hotel (very expensive) and taxi service of a sort. Nordair has a base here with a hangar, and their personnel are very helpful to visiting pilots. Fuel is Esso; the landing fee is minimal, and there are instrument approaches. I, personally, would be sure that the weather to Sondrestrom was going to be good the next day before coming to Frobisher! I can think of more interesting places to be weathered in (Figure 10-3).

FIGURE 10-2
Frobisher Bay's buildings are at the right of the single runway.

FIGURE 10-3
If you spend the night in a $50 hotel room, this is what you can see from your window at the end of May.

From Frobisher it is 480 nautical miles across Baffin Island and Davis Strait to Sondre Stromfjord with the ice floes and icebergs in the strait and spectacular scenery of Greenland and its fjords, mountains, and icecap as we wend our way up the fjord to Sondrestrom airport. This is a joint-use airport for the Danish and United States military and also airline and general aviation airplanes. The large terminal on the civilian side of the runway contains a good hotel on its upper stories, as well as the Met Office, Control Office, cafeteria, etc. (Figure 10-4). Fuel is Esso; landing fees are large and variable (I have paid from $51 to $93). There are

FIGURE 10-4

Sondrestrom airport. Parking and services are on the North side of the runway. The Danish Terminal Building and its second-floor hotel are in the background.

not only instrument approaches but also radar. There is no hangar available unless you have a friend in the USAF; and you should not count on too much in the way of maintenance, as the mechanics are either airline or military personnel.

If you are a United States citizen, you will probably have to get permission from the USAF to land here (this depends on the current commanding officer; there have been times when I could go in with no problems, and other times not). This requires 30 days' notice, an AF Form 181, a Hold Harmless Agreement, and an AF Form 203 Certificate of Insurance from your insurance carrier, affirming that you have the required insurance. If you are a citizen of another country, none of this is necessary!

It would be a great pity to stop here only for fuel. Greenland is a fascinating country with a long history, and many interesting things to do and see. For fishermen, I'm told, it is fantastic, with salmon, cod, and arctic char; there are also shrimp, whales, and seal. For history buffs there are settlements and ruins from all periods back to 500 B.C., when the Eskimos arrived. Eric the Red came from Iceland in A.D. 986 with fourteen ships and started several settlements; Dutch, British, Norwegian, and Danish whalers put in at various points along the West coast and left their mark back in the 1700s and 1800s.

It is possible to watch the Eskimos build kayaks and make all their unique handicrafts (and of course, you can buy them, too). Tours are available by boat or helicopter to most of the towns and settlements and are something none of your friends can brag about.

The airway from Sondrestrom across the icecap to Kulusuk on the East coast has a minimum enroute altitude of 11,000 feet; the distance is 345 nautical miles. The route goes past a radar site which is called Sea Bass. It is not necessary to talk to them, but it is a good idea and you will find them happy to have a conversation with a pilot of a small plane. When you see that little black dot with only ice around for hundreds of miles, you'll understand.

Kulusuk airport is on an island off the coast at Angmagssalik. It has a published NDB approach of rather unusual shape, and Icelandair is trying to build a tourist business in this area. The town is on the mainland, and there is overnight accommodation. More and more Europe? going there for hiking in the mountains and among ciers. Weather information comes from Sondrestrom, and one must be very sure of good weather before going there.

Kulusuk to Reykjavik is 380 nautical miles across the Denmark Strait and overheading Keflavik, 20 miles West of Reykjavik. The Keflavik VOR can be picked up about 120 miles out, but there is a very strong broadcast station in Reykjavik on 209 kilohertz; one can receive this station just past Kulusuk.

Keflavik is a joint-use airport, but while it has good radar and approaches, as well as fuel and weather information (and a duty-free shop), you must go to Reykjavik to sleep, so you might as well land at Reykjavik in the first place.

Reykjavik is a good airport and also has instrument approaches and radar; the Lofleidir Hotel is right on the field, so you can look out your window at your airplane (Figures 10-5 to 10-7). The personnel of the Assisting Office will meet your plane and arrange for fuel, hotel reservations, weather

FIGURE 10-5
Reykjavik is the capital and largest city of Iceland. The Lutheran Cathedral is the outstanding feature of its skyline and seems fairly close to your wing tip on landing Runway 20.

FIGURE 10-6
Reykjavik airport from above. It has water on two sides and city on the other two sides. One can walk into the city.

FIGURE 10-7
Reykjavik Runway 20 on approach. The large buildings to the left of the runway house the Tower and ATC and the Lofleidir Hotel.

information, and flight-plan filing. Fuel is BP or Shell; BP must be paid for in Icelandic krónur but is several cents cheaper than Shell, for which you can use either cash or an International Carnet. Landing fees are fairly high, ranging from about $30 to $65, depending on the type of aircraft. Normally, there is no hangar space available, but in an emergency you could talk your way into the hangar. Maintenance is excellent, although parts for your bird may not be available. The airplanes based there are mostly Piper Cherokees and Cessna 150s and 172s.

Again, one should not leave Iceland unseen; however, I will save the arguments in its favor for later in the chapter, and we will proceed to the Faroe Islands.

The route from Reykjavik goes East across the southern part of Iceland with spectacular glaciers and volcanos (dead and not so dead) on both sides reaching up 6000 to 7000 feet. We leave the coast at Ingolfshofoi VOR on course for Vagar in the Faroe Islands; the distance is 430 nautical miles. Sorvag/Vagar airport is operative only between 9 A.M. and 5 P.M. Fuel is available, but since quantities are limited, it will be wise to check before going. There is radar and an NDB for approach. The Faroe Islands belong to Denmark so the food is good. They are interesting little islands with beautiful scenery and well worth spending a couple of days.

From Vagar the course to Stornoway in Scotland is almost due South and the distance is 225 nautical miles; or you can continue down to Prestwick or Glasgow, which are about 400 nautical miles from Vagar.

Now we have crossed the Atlantic Ocean, arrived on the East side of it, and have all Europe before us for exploring. The plotting chart for this route is Aircraft Position Chart 3097, obtainable from National Ocean Survey in Riverdale, Maryland. Also needed are ONC charts and Low Altitude Radio Facility charts, obtainable from the same place or from Jeppesen Company.

If your airplane has a normal cruising range of 900 to 1000 nautical miles, you may wish to use the route which goes through Goose Bay, Labrador; Narssarssuaq, Greenland; Reykjavik, Iceland; and down to Prestwick, Scotland, thus making fewer stops. The longest leg on this route is 740 nautical miles from Reykjavik to Prestwick, but of course, Stornoway is 150 miles closer as an alternate.

From Presque Isle, Maine, to Goose Bay is 530 nautical miles. If we are on a VFR flight plan, we can go direct across the Gaspé Peninsula and the Northern tip of Anticosti Island in the Gulf of St. Lawrence, and on over the uninhabited lakes and forests of Labrador. If we are on an IFR flight plan, the route will take us up to Mont Joli and diagonally across the St. Lawrence River to Sept Îles and from there past the emergency strip and NDB at Lake Eon on into Goose. Except for the Lake Eon strip there is practically no sign of man for hundreds of miles in this part of the world. Goose Bay itself is not hard to find because it lies at the southwest end of Lake Melville, which opens out from Hamilton Inlet coming in from the ocean.

Try not to get weathered in at Goose; it really is dismal, especially in bad weather. There is a new hotel on the "Base," which is now operated by the Canadian government since the United States Air Force pulled out. The Weather Office and the Flight Service Station are also here, and the taxi rides to and from the airplane are much shorter than from Happy Valley.

Airport fees are minimal although Customs charges $30 if you come in after hours or on weekends. Fuel is Esso; there is no hangar space and little service, but Nordair has a base here also and their personnel are quite helpful, just as they are at Frobisher.

From Goose the route goes out to the coast 100 miles away along Lake Melville and Hamilton Inlet; from the coast, by which time we have lost the Goose VOR if we are at 9000 feet, we continue across 500 miles of water to the island of Simiutak (Figure 10-8). The NDB on Simiutak is quite strong and can be used from about halfway across. You are expected to contact Julienahaab radio on frequency 118.1 at least 150 miles before reaching Simiutak. It is a good idea so that Julienahaab can contact Narssarssuaq to advise them of your imminent arrival and also get the latest weather for you. Julienahaab is on the coast, which makes it possible to talk to them long before you can reach Narssarssuaq at the end of the fjord.

FIGURE 10-8
Simiutak is the largest of a group of islands in this area of the West coast of Greenland, and here is the NDB toward which we have been aiming. From here a Magnetic Heading of 089° will lead to the correct fjord of the three we see ahead (the middle one).

Three fjords are visible from the island of Simiutak, and the middle one has Narssarssuaq at its far end, so be sure to leave the NDB on a Magnetic Heading of 089° as the fjord to the right dead-ends into a glacier and the one to the left dead-ends into a 3000-foot hill. If the weather is good, you can jump over this hill to find the airport. Narssarssauq's fjord is 45 miles long and not completely straight. About 20 miles in at the base of the first big hill on your left is the fair-sized (for Greenland) town of Narssaq (Figure 10-9); from there you will see a round hill jutting out from the left side under a rather high mountain (Figure 10-10); behind this round hill is a sunken freighter (Figure 10-11), which will identify the fjord absolutely. Shortly after you pass the

FIGURE 10-9
Looking up the fjord, we see a string of islands on the left leading to a cliff, under which is the town of Narssaq. Beyond we can just see where the fjord curves to the right around a small hill.

FIGURE 10-10
Here is the small round hill around which the fjord in Figure 10-9 is curving. For what is on the other side, see Figure 10-11.

ship, the fjord swing to the left around the mountain (Figure 10-12); as you make this turn, be ready to land because the runway will be immediately on the right (Figure 10-13). It also ends in a glacier, so go-arounds are not recommended. The valley containing the airport is very narrow, with 3000- to 7000-foot mountains on three sides, and the airport is only for VFR daylight use.

FIGURE 10-11

The sunken freighter which, since the first airplane flew in here during World War II, has identified this fjord beyond doubt.

Fuel is Esso and fairly expensive; landing fees range from $30 up, depending on the type of airplane. There is a Weather Office and Flight-Plan Service, but communication difficulties sometimes interfere with acquisition of information and transmission of flight plans.

In planning a flight to Narssarssuaq one must be cautious about the weather forecast as the nearest alternate is Sondrestrom, which is 385 nautical miles North and probably out of reach. If the surface and lower altitude winds are from the Southwest, be a bit suspicious; a wind from that direction is blowing up the fjord from the sea and tends to bring low clouds and fog at the fjord mouth. Trying to sneak up the fjord under a low ceiling with poor visibility is guaranteed to give one gray hair at the very least; trying to spiral down from overhead the airport into the bowl of mountains is not any better.

Having made as sure as possible that the weather is and will remain good until arrival, the next important item is to

FIGURE 10-12
As you follow the fjord left around this mountain, prepare for landing. The runway will appear immediately on the right with a glacier at the other end, so don't overshoot.

plan the flight to arrive between 8 A.M. and 4 P.M. Monday through Friday. Arrival after 4 P.M. will cost an *extra* $100; arrival (or departure) on Saturday or Sunday will cost an *extra* $300. The Danish government has decided that pilots are a nuisance and should be milked freely. The people who live and work at Narssarssuaq are unhappy about this because they lead a confined life and visiting pilots are always welcomed; however, they have no choice but to collect the money for their government.

FIGURE 10-13

The runway at Narssarssuaq is fairly well hemmed in and slopes slightly uphill toward the glacier at the East end. Landings are normally made to the East and takeoffs to the West.

In summer the Hotel Arctic operates with personnel and amenities brought from Denmark, and there are a number of airline flights from Denmark and Iceland bringing tourists to Greenland. The hotel is comfortable and the food is very good. Many activities are provided for visitors; one can join a group hiking up the glacier off the end of the runway, do some salmon fishing, take a boat across the fjord to visit Leif Ericsson's settlement, or ride a boat or a helicopter down the fjord and to the various towns along the coast and up in the fjords of the West coast (Figure 10-14). Try not to leave without seeing some of these interesting things.

After the summer is over at the end of August, the accommodations are in the same buildings, but one eats in the mess with the employees and residents of the airport settlement. The food, of course, is still good, but the meal hours are more restricted.

FIGURE 10-14
Icebergs like this one (which is taller than it seems) can be obstructions just off the approach to Narssarssuaq during the summer. On the opposite shore are the remains of Leif Ericsson's original settlement.

Leaving Narssarssuaq for Reykjavik, one climbs to 8000 feet either over the airport (Figure 10-15) or down the fjord and back before departing the NDB eastbound over the ice-cap. The minimum altitude is 11,000 feet as there are 9000-foot mountains on both sides of the track. There is no other word than spectacular for Greenland and its mountains, fjords, and icecap. Be sure to take a camera and plenty of film.

We leave the coast of Greenland 90 miles to the East to cross 550 miles of ocean to Keflavik on the Southwest corner of Iceland. The Reykjavik broadcast station on 209 kilohertz will cause the ADF needle to point shortly after we pass 40° West, and at 34° West we are in Iceland's control area.

There is no better way to see Iceland than from your own airplane. Almost every town around the coast has an airstrip; some of them are small, but adequate for the aircraft which serve them. In winter all travel must be by air. I have always found the people hospitable and eager to show the visitor the local sights. The atmosphere of Iceland is marvelously clear because heat and hot water come from hot springs with the steam piped to the towns, and electricity is

FIGURE 10-15

Narssarssuaq seen from the air while climbing to cruise altitude.

generated by the myriad waterfalls on every river as it drops on its way from the interior plateau to the sea. The scenery is composed of glaciers and volcanos, moonscapes of lava (the astronauts did some of their moon training here), geysirs and sulfur lakes, bubbling hot springs, sheep farms, and a whaling station. The coast is indented by hundreds of beautiful fjords.

In all the larger towns as well as in the capital, Reykjavik, there are good hotels.

The Vestmann Islands, which lie 70 miles Southeast of Reykjavik, are also worth a visit. The main island of Heimay has an airport and regular service from Reykjavik (Figure 10-16). Fishing and fish processing are the chief industries on the island; at certain times of the year puffins and their eggs also provide a change for the diet. In January 1973 an eruption occurred on the north face of the volcano of Helgafell, between the town and the airport. This eruption buried part of the town of Heimay and changed the shape of the island and its harbor (Figure 10-17). It is called Kirk-

FIGURE 10-16
The town of Heimay on the main island of the Vestmanns, with its well-protected harbor for the fishing fleet.

ufell because it formed another mountain over the principal church of the town (Figure 10-18). A few miles West of Heimay a new island erupted from the sea in 1969, which is called Surtsey. It is uninhabited, and scientists are using it as a laboratory to discover how life begins in a completely sterile area.

FIGURE 10-17
Heimay a few months after the eruption, with most of the town covered with lava, which is still flowing into the harbor.

FIGURE 10-18
Kirkufell and its steam and flowing lava 3 months after the initial eruption.

From the Vestmann Island NDB it is just over 500 nautical miles to Stornoway on the Isle of Lewis in the Outer
Hebrides of Scotland or to Benbecula VOR on the island of
Benbecula if your destination is Prestwick. Prestwick is on
the West coast of Scotland, and the airport has all necessary
services as it is an International Airport. Be prepared for
tight security and long walks from one office to another.
Just up the hill from the airport is a delightful small hotel,
Towans, which is in easy walking distance (if your suitcase
is not heavy); the Martin family who run it are very hospitable to pilots.

*   *   *

If you have installed long-range tanks in your airplane,
you may want to go direct from either Goose Bay or Gander
to Reykjavik. From Goose the distance is 1330 nautical
miles in a fairly straight line and passing the NDB at Prince
Christian on the Southeast tip of Greenland (Figures 10-19
to 10-21). From Gander the distance is 1420 nautical miles

FIGURE 10-19
*Approaching the Southern tip of Greenland in the summer,
when the ice has broken and moves out of the fjords in the
form of floes and icebergs.*

FIGURE 10-20

The intensely clear blue water of the fjords is so still that one can hardly distinguish between mountains and reflections.

FIGURE 10-21

A little way up on the East coast, Prince Christian NDB and its caretakers are nestled against the mountain in the mouth of the fjord, invisible under the snow in winter.

with a slight jog to cross Prince Christian. It always seems good to me to have a spot along the route where I am absolutely positive of my position, and Prince Christian provides this at approximately the halfway point. This also gives a sure check on groundspeed, and therefore the actual wind encountered. If you discover at this point that the wind is spoiling your time estimates, you can still return to Gander or Goose or go to Narssarssuaq (if its weather is good) rather than take a chance on even more adverse winds, with the possibility of running short of fuel. It is *very* cold water to ditch in.

SHANNON IS A LONG WAY ACROSS

The most direct route from the United States to Europe is of course from Boston to Gander and across to Shannon in Ireland. Although the ocean leg is longer than any of the others, the overall distance is an approximation of the Great Circle and is therefore shorter to any city of Europe.

From Boston to Gander is 800 nautical miles, 230 miles across water to Yarmouth at the Southwest tip of Nova Sco-

FIGURE 10-22
Gander airport and its associated town are the only signs of civilization in the wilderness.

tia and then along the peninsula past Halifax to Sydney on Cape Breton Island, and from Sydney across the Gulf of St. Lawrence to Ramea Island and across Newfoundland to Gander (Figures 10-22 and 10-23).

Halifax is a good stop as it is an international airport so Customs is available at all times. There is a weather forecast office at Halifax and usually hangar space either at the Flying Club or the fixed base operator. Radar and instrument approaches, of course. The only hitch is that any overnight accommodations are about 25 miles away in Dartmouth or Halifax; this has caused me to spend the night on a bench at the airport on occasion.

Sydney is better if one needs maintenance, as Eastern Flying Service has a shop with helpful mechanics; however Customs charges to come out from town after normal working hours. The city of Sydney is only a few miles away, and I've always succeeded in finding a room.

FIGURE 10-23
Gander's beautiful Terminal and the smallest airplane I ferried (this one to Switzerland) under the wing of a "Pregnant Guppy" of NASA.

Stephenville on the West coast of Newfoundland is a poor stop on all counts. The airport people are friendly, but accommodations are rather bad and fueling, checking the weather, and filing the flight plan all are difficult.

St. John's, Newfoundland, is a good stop and also a good departure point except for its weather, which can be bad when everybody else's is good. Customs is always available, and fuel, hangar space, and maintenance are all available with Innotech Aviation across the field from the terminal. The Airport Inn is only about a mile away and there is a Holiday Inn about 3 miles down the road. If you stay at St. John's, Stephenville, or Sydney, you will be requesting your ocean weather information from the Gander Weather Office either by teletype or telephone.

Gander's chief attraction is the Weather Office, as there is no hangar or maintenance available. In a dire emergency Allied Aviation can sometimes be persuaded to help out, but they do not like to work on private airplanes and their prices are horrendous. Allied is airline-owned—nuff said!

The town of Gander is 2 miles from the airport and therefore close enough to walk if you are stuck and want something to occupy the time. There is not much else to do; there are several hotel-motels. Both the town and the airport are on the Eastern shore of Gander Lake; the shores of the lake are about 200 feet above the water surface, so if you are making an approach to Runway 4 be alert for turbulence from the outer marker to the runway, as the wind sweeps down to the water and back up the West side.

Forty-two miles out from Gander airport on the Great Circle route to Shannon is an NDB at Wesleyville on the coast. I always plan to reach my cruising altitude of 9000 feet (FL090) by this point; it makes it easier to estimate track and groundspeed from a definite spot.

We will cross the coast of Ireland 1630 nautical miles later at the mouth of the Shannon River. This route definitely requires some method of navigation other than dead reckoning and ADF. The ICAO mandates that all aircraft in the airspace above 27,500 feet (FL275) have two independent systems, which can be Inertial, Omega, Doppler, VLF, or any combination of them. These systems are out of sight for smaller airplanes from the point of view of cost, size, weight, and installation problems. However, for the smaller airplanes in the lower levels Loran C is available to buy for less than $3000 or to rent for a given trip. Texas Instruments has a set designed for boats but which works beautifully in airplanes; its size is right, it weighs only 9 pounds, and it can be tied into the HF antenna. Being completely automatic, it is simple to use.

Shannon is not a town; it is an international airport and industrial park (Figures 10-24 and 10-25). Since it is an international airport, Customs and Immigration, fuel, and weather information are all available 24 hours a day. You will need your raincoat and your walking shoes as the light-

FIGURE 10-24
Seventeen hundred nautical miles out of Gander we arrive at the airport of Shannon, Ireland, on the River Shannon. The buildings on the perimeter are part of its industrial park, and many of the companies are American.

FIGURE 10-25
The Control Tower and Maintenance Buildings at Shannon.

aircraft park is a long way from the new Terminal. The Terminal itself is large, with the services you need all in different directions. The Shannon Repair Services hangar and shop give quite good maintenance and can remove and reinstall your tanks should you wish to fly around Europe without them. The red tape involved in removal and reinstallation is very much less here than anywhere else. Fuel is Shell, and unless you have an International Carnet, it must be paid for in Irish cash. (The dollar has been varying too much lately.) There is a currency exchange in the Terminal.

Across the street from the Terminal is the Shannon International Hotel, which is very comfortable although it no longer serves any meals except breakfast; the other meals can be had in the Terminal in either the cafeteria or the restaurant. Ireland is well worth seeing as it is a lovely green country; at least take one of the many bus tours from the hotel and try the medieval banquet at Bunratty Castle not far from the airport. There are all sorts of fascinating things to see and do in Ireland either in your own airplane or by road, but this is not supposed to be a travelog. Most of my sightseeing has been done on weekends while waiting for a business day to deliver the airplane that brought me here.

HOW ABOUT THE AZORES?

Even with long-range tanks installed, it may happen that the wind and/or weather forecast for the Shannon or Iceland routes will not be such that you wish to tackle it. In such a case, Santa Maria in the Azores could be your choice to avoid sitting around Gander waiting for an improvement on the other routes. From Gander the route goes Southeast over St. John's and then to Flores Island and through the islands to Santa Maria. The total distance is 1510 nautical miles.

The pilot flying to Santa Maria needs to be able to navigate with Loran C as much as the pilot on the Shannon route, although not for as long a distance. If you miss the islands, the coast of Europe is another 750 miles away. From St. John's it is 1050 nautical miles to Flores Island; however, the St. John's VOR will hold for about 90 miles and the Flores NDB will be usable for 150 miles or so. This leaves a little more than 800 miles for Loran C navigating. From Flores the airway goes to the NDB on Gracioso, from there to the VOR on Terceira, thence to the NDB on San Miguel, and down to the VOR at Santa Maria.

These are semitropical islands so they usually have a cover of big cumulus clouds. Santa Maria Control is very firm about HF radio. If you have not talked to them on the way in, you will not be allowed to leave until you prove that your HF is working. If it is not, you stay until it is fixed unless another airplane comes along and can be persuaded to fly in company with you to give position reports for both airplanes. If you are flying a jet or a turbo-prop in the upper levels, you may be able to persuade the Chief Controller that VHF will be readable all the way. Good Luck!

Lajes Air Base on the island of Terceira may look tempting but being a military base for both the United States and Portugal, it is definitely off limits and for emergency only; *and* the emergency had better be a real one. Santa Maria is an international airport with Customs and Immigration, fuel, and weather available around the clock (Figures 10-26 and 10-27). All the airport personnel work 12-hour shifts, but there is not much traffic, so if you arrive or depart in the middle of the night, you must wake people up; they all have a place for sleeping between airplane arrivals or departures. There is a big blackboard in the operations office where all inbound and outbound flights are posted with the times of departure from Gander or wherever and the estimated time of arrival at Santa Maria.

Although the runway is lighted all night, if you land or take off when the lights are on, you pay $10 to use them. Fuel is subject to Customs fees, and since it is a flat fee, the more you buy the cheaper it is by the liter. Shell and Esso both come out of the same pit with different pumper wagons. Airport fees vary according to the time of day and

FIGURE 10-26
Santa Maria is the Southernmost island of the Azores. The only
flat spot is on the Western side, where the airport is. The
cliffs off three sides rise sheer to 305 feet above sea level.
Runway 01/19 is the preferred one, but small airplanes need
Runway 30 when the wind is strong from the West because of
the turbulence from the cliffs.

FIGURE 10-27
The Terminal on Santa Maria is long and low. The island
climbs rapidly to the East into the mountains seen in
the background.

the type of aircraft and run from $25 up. Maintenace is very
good as long as no parts are needed; the mechanics work for
the local airline, SATA, and are meticulous in their work.

The Azores are seven volcanic islands lying 700 nautical
miles West of Portugal, to which they belong. Since they
are semitropical, all kinds of fruits and vegetables grow in

profusioń, including the most delicious pineapples I have ever eaten. The tea plantations on the island of San Miguel are extensive and quite beautiful. As in all islands, fish of all kinds are plentiful and cooked in a variety of interesting ways.

All the islands are worth a visit, as each one has its own character and customs. There are many Saints, and one can almost always find a delightful village fiesta celebrating some Saint's day with everybody dressed in traditional costumes and the clergy in their finest richly embroidered and colorful vestments. Portuguese people are warm and friendly, and the language barrier seems not to exist because they are adept at guessing what you mean without words. Their handiwork in metals and embroidery is exquisite.

Leaving Santa Maria for the mainland of Europe, one can go to Lisbon, Portugal, which is a beautiful city (Figure 10-28); or if your destination is more Northerly, go to the Northwest corner of Spain to Santiago, where there is a very beautiful Cathedral with a fascinating history as well as a large University.

FIGURE 10-28
Lisbon is situated on the curve of the Tagus River, where it bends to the Southwest to enter the Atlantic. The airport can be seen in the background and the river and harbor in the near foreground.

GENERAL INFORMATION

Routes discussed in this chapter are shown in Figure 10-29. For the route through Frobisher and Sondrestrom use Aircraft Position Chart 3097. For the other routes use Aircraft Position Chart 3071 with Loran C information. Radio Facility Charts and Supplements and approach plates are necessary; ONC charts are helpful for land areas. Reykjavik broadcast station on 209 kilohertz is usable for 400 or more miles to the West; it is less useful to the South, as there is another station on the same frequency in the Eastern part of Iceland.

Athlone broadcast station, 55 miles North-Northeast of Shannon on 565.5 kilohertz, is useful for about 500 to 600 miles. The BBC at Birmingham on 200 kilohertz is useful up to 1000 miles. The Lisbon broadcast stations on 355, 665, and 755 kilohertz can be used for 400 to 600 nautical miles.

On any route it is well to carry your own chocks as there are usually no chocks or tie-downs available anywhere.

FIGURE 10-29(a)
The Northern routes on Aircraft Position Chart 3097. Major points enroute are 1 Sept Îles, 2 Fort Chimo,
3 Frobisher, 4 Sondrestrom AB, 5 Kulusuk,
6 Reykjavik, 7 Faroe Islands, 8 Goose Bay,
9 Narssarssuaq, and 10 Stornoway.

FIGURE 10-29(b)
The Central and Southern routes on Aircraft Position Chart 3071. Major points enroute are. 1 Gander, 2 Shannon,
3 St. John's, 4 Flores, 5 Lajes AFB, 6 Santa Maria
7 Lisbon, and 8 Santiago.

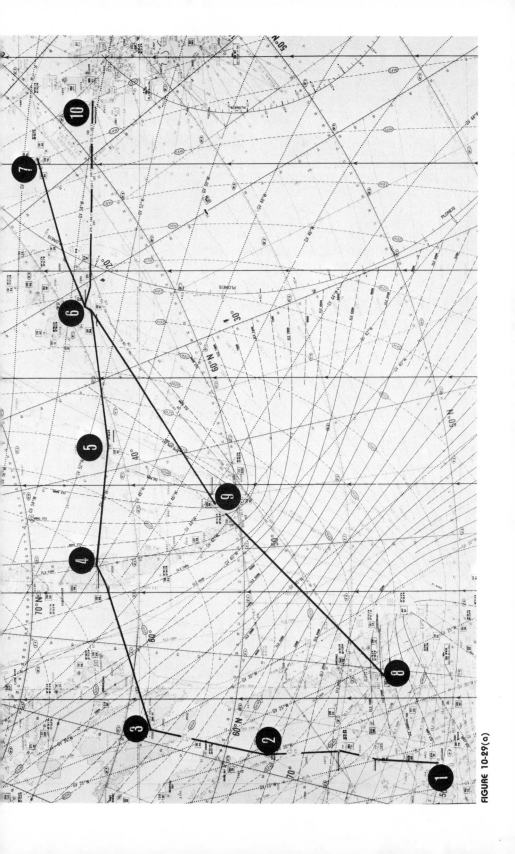

FIGURE 10-29(a)

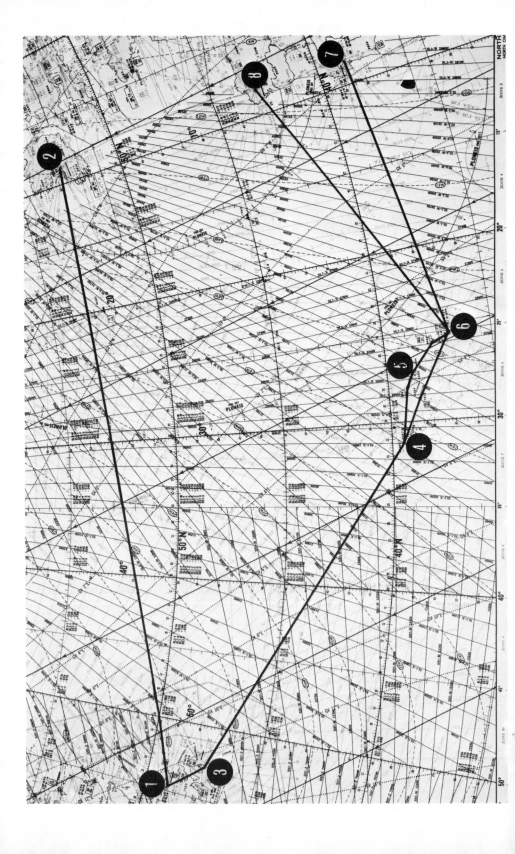

11 Route Characteristics of the Pacific

The Pacific Ocean is quite different from the Atlantic in several ways. The distances are much greater and the choice of routes much smaller; the weather generally is better and the winds lighter, but we are in more tropical latitudes most of the time, so we encounter more tropical storms and there are more typhoons to avoid.

The most frequently used route is from the San Francisco area to Hawaii, either Honolulu or Hilo on the Big Island, and from there to wherever is our destination. It is sometimes possible to go to the Aleutians and from there down to some island of our choice. Of this route I can say nothing because each time I have planned to use it the weather has been impossible; there seems to be fog in the Aleutians a great percentage of the time throughout the year.

The San Francisco area is the closest point on the mainland to the Hawaiian Islands. If you have the equipment required to enter and leave from a Class 1 TCA, then San Francisco itself is the obvious choice as a departure point, because the Weather Bureau and the forecasters who are concerned with the ocean are there; it is always helpful to be able to look at the charts and the satellite pictures yourself. If the TCA is a problem, San Jose airport at the bottom of the Bay is a good departure point and the General Aviation Terminal personnel are quite helpful. Leaving from here, one can skirt the TCA without trouble. As anyone who has been in the Bay area knows, fog in the early morning is a continuing problem. This means that the time of takeoff is dictated more by the fog than by the pilot's desires in many cases.

I well remember a February morning when I had planned to leave San Jose at daybreak, which was 0700. When I checked the weather the night before, I was told that there was a very good possibility of fog starting about 0600 and lasting until at least 1000. This didn't sound good so I set the alarm for 0400 and called again; the forecaster said it would certainly be foggy by 0600, and probably earlier. I hurried everything as much as one can at that hour of the morning, but as I started the takeoff roll at 0515 the fog was already at the other end of the runway.

San Francisco is like Santa Maria in the Azores in that they are adamant that your HF radio *must* be working; they require a test call shortly after you leave the coast and will order you back if this call is unsuccessful. This is for your own safety, of course, but be sure that the HF is working before arriving in the San Francisco area so that you don't have to waste time there getting it fixed or replaced.

A few years ago I arrived in San Francisco with what had been the correct frequencies only 3 months before. Now they had been changed, and it was necessary that I have at least one of the new frequencies. There are several radio shops on Oakland airport; I had to go from one to another until I found a set of crystals. The shop was busy and said they could not install them for me for 2 days. Fortunately I had had some experience in changing crystals on these older HF radios, so I did it myself. Nowadays that would not be possible as the Sideband radios cannot be changed so simply.

*   *   *

After departure we leave the coast fairly quickly and have about 2000 nautical miles of water to traverse before seeing land once again. The Oakland and Point Reyes VORs are quite strong and give a good departure; also the broadcast station on 680 kilohertz, which is about 8 miles South of San Francisco, is powerful enough for reception up to 500 miles out. Loran should be required equipment even more out here, where we are aiming for an island, than it is on the Atlantic, where we are aiming for a continent. The coastal chain is usable for almost 1200 miles toward Hawaii, and the Hawaiian chain comes in about 600 miles out, so there is only 300 miles without some help besides dead reckoning. There are several strong broadcast stations on the islands, particularly on Oahu, which will activate our ADF about 600 miles out, and the island VORs seem to have better than normal line-of-sight range. Most of the way the clouds will be broken variable to scattered with tops below 6000 feet. The probability of a tailwind is not very good, so the fuel supply must be enough to go 2200 nautical miles with a 10-knot headwind and still have a reserve. For this, most airplanes will be 20 to 25 percent over gross weight, requiring a special FAA permit and special care on takeoff and climb as performance suffers to some extent.

Wind forecasts need to be questioned very carefully on this route as the North side of a High and the South side of a Low will definitely give one a headwind; the pressure gradient will determine its strength. Also be wary of crosswinds because, unless you are using Loran for navigation you can drift a long way in 2000 miles; each degree of drift will equal 30 miles before you receive any usable radio signals from the islands.

Several years ago, while Ocean Station November was still out there at the halfway point, I did not receive her NDB when I should have. I asked an airliner overhead to find out if it was operating and the answer was "yes." When my time for passing her had arrived and still no reception (I should have received it 150 miles away), I realized I must have drifted either North or South of my track by quite a lot. It was a single-engine airplane, so I still had plenty of fuel. I flew South for 30 minutes, and then North for 1 hour 5 minutes, but still nothing. Obviously, I was a great distance off course with no knowledge of which direction, so my chances of arriving at Honolulu seemed to me to be slender.

Much as I hated to waste the fuel and time, I felt that returning would prevent a long swim, so I advised San Francisco that I had reversed course. They were quite upset and thought I was short of fuel even though I kept assuring them that such was not the case; it was a matter of not knowing where I was. Eventually I picked up the radio station on 680 kilohertz, and from the bearing of it I realized that I must have been about 250 miles South of my track. The wind had been almost 180° different from the forecast wind. Two days before that little contretemps another ferry pilot had also missed "November," kept on going, and went into the drink too far away to be found. Immediately there was a notice posted that if an aircraft did not have contact with "November," it must return. "November" is no longer there, so. . . .

There is quite a lot of airline traffic between the mainland and Hawaii and these crews are very friendly and helpful to the small planes "down there." One day my Loran A reception was poor, and it seemed to me I had been sitting and going nowhere for much too long. Overhead I saw a beautiful contrail so I called, "Aircraft in the vicinity of 2530 North 150 West, do you read Sacchi 230 on one two one five?"

There were two answers, one from United and one from American. I only saw one contrail and so stated.

United said,

"It's probably us you see. We will make a forty-five degree turn and you can tell by the contrail."

They did, and it was them; when they gave me their position it developed that I was OK, just impatient. So I thanked them and continued on with some relief. I often wondered what the passengers thought about the turn in the middle of the ocean, but maybe they didn't even notice it.

By the time you reach 155° West, it is possible to begin looking for cross bearings from the NDBs and VORs of the islands you will be passing on your way to either Honolulu or Hilo, and soon you will be on a Victor airway again. The islands, as they rise out of the blue sea, are truly beautiful whether they have caps of cumulus clouds so that the peaks are hidden, or whether they lie cloudless under the sun with their unbelievably varying shades of green surrounded by white beaches with the surf of the blue, blue sea lapping the shore. It is always a temptation to descend to a low altitude and fly around each island, but restrain yourself, as Honolulu control would be very unhappy. Plan to stay over and do this another day.

Both Honolulu and Hilo have all the services one needs, so it is only a matter of which island one prefers or what the next destination may be (Figure 11-1). If we are Westbound to Wake or Majuro, the distance is shorter from Honolulu; if Southbound to Pago Pago in American Samoa, the distance is shorter from Hilo.

From Honolulu through Wake or Majuro (Wake is sometimes out of action from damage by typhoons) and Guam to Manila and the Orient, we are below 20° North latitude. This means that we are in the domain of the Northeast Trades, so the wind will be out of the East or Northeast and

FIGURE 11-1
The main runway at Honolulu International/Hickman Field on approach from the West over the entrance to Pearl Harbor. The Main Terminal is to the left and General Aviation services at the east end of the runway.

FIGURE 11-2
The friendly cloud columns of good weather over the Pacific. A very light wind makes the Eastward lean hardly noticeable. The dark area in the upper left is the chart I tape on the windows to keep the tropical sun off me.

usually fairly light. For the pilot it is interesting to know that the wind is stronger down near the surface than it is at 6000 or 8000 feet; it is also very hot and bumpy down near the surface! The clouds will be scattered towers of cumulus with tops between 6000 and 12,000 feet, except when the weather is bad (Figure 11-2). This means that the cloud tops are leaning toward the East, and in more Northern regions would indicate a headwind if you are Westbound. However, in the Trade Wind belt it only means a stronger tailwind at lower altitude if Westbound or a stronger headwind if Eastbound at lower altitude.

In ancient days, the Polynesians navigated from island to island partly by observing that an island almost always had a cumulus cloud over it. We can do the same today because in normal weather in these latitudes most frequently the only really large cumulus clouds are those hiding an island under them. After we have flown for 2000 nautical miles from Honolulu, we will see a large cloud; then we know that we will very soon see that welcome and lovely sight of a pale green lagoon surrounded by the white coral reefs with the blue Pacific all around, which is Wake Island. We have, of course, been using our Loran for navigation, and about 800 miles back we began to pick up the Wake NDB on the ADF, but this little dot of green and white in the middle of all that blue is certainly exciting (Figure 11-3). Wake is available for landing or takeoff only between 8 A.M. and 4 P.M. local time, which is 12 hours ahead of GMT, or Zulu, time because we have crossed the International Date Line, and it is tomorrow.

If Wake becomes unusable because of typhoon damage or if an Aleutian Low causes headwinds, one must go to Majuro in the Marshall Islands (Figure 11-4). This is the only island available for civilians. The distance from Honolulu is about 2100 miles, and it lies 800 miles South-Southeast of Wake. Majuro is more expensive than Wake, and the overnight accommodations may not be as good.

FIGURE 11-3
The welcome sight of Wake Island too early in the day for cumulus buildups. The airstrip and tank farm are on the right, and living quarters are coyly hiding under the clouds.

FIGURE 11-4
Majuro islanders turned out en masse to see the first small airplanes to land on this strip in January 1968. Since then the runway, facilities, and accommodations have been improved.

From either Wake or Majuro the next stop will be Guam or Saipan. Either one will require prior permission—in fact any of the Pacific Islands do, but Guam is a Navy Base (Figure 11-5) and one needs the same paperwork we discussed for Sondrestrom, except that this is Navy paperwork rather than Air Force.

Guam is quite a large island, being 30 miles long and from 4 to 8 miles wide. It is the seat of government for the Trust Territories and has a very interesting history going back several thousand years. It was one of the islands much fought over during the war and in the last few years has become a popular destination for Japanese tourists, particularly honeymooners, so there are new hotels going up all over the island, many of them built and run by Japanese. One can

FIGURE 11-5
The Naval Air Station at Agana, Guam, lies on a plateau above the town. There are always rain showers over Guam, but beneath the clouds the town and Western coast are visible.

have a pleasant stay here with all sorts of sports available and wonderful beaches for sunning or swimming. There are many things to see: the Latte Stones, which are part of the mystery of the early Pacific peoples (as are the ruins on Ponape, the ancient stone weirs on Yap, the stone temples on Malden, and the Latte Stones on Rota and Tinian). There are also remains of old Spanish churches and forts, and of course, the ruins of Japanese fortifications from World War II.

   Should you prefer to go to Saipan (Figure 11-6) which is about 100 miles North of Guam, you will also need prior permission from the Saipan authorities. Fuel is only sold by the drum, is pumped by hand into the airplane, and is quite expensive. This island is interesting because many of the Japanese fortifications and hideouts are left. The biggest hill on the island (Figure 11-7) is honeycombed with their caves, and the Saipanese can tell some gruesome stories of the war.

FIGURE 11-6
Saipan was much fought over during World War II. To the left of the new airport are old revetments and ammunition dumps.

FIGURE 11-7
The old runway of Saipan with revetments and dumps in the foreground. The mountain in the background is honeycombed with Japanese caves.

From Guam to Manila is almost 1400 nautical miles and from Saipan it is 1440 nautical miles. You will come to the Eastern part of the island of Luzon about 100 miles before reaching Manila, and the VOR at Jomalig is quite strong. The Philippines are still under martial law as of 1978, so be very careful that you have the required permissions for everything as well as a visa in your passport. Manila is an international airport so that all services are available and there are dealers on the field for most makes of airplanes.

Manila is a good gateway to the rest of Asia, or at least those parts of it which are open to civilian airplanes.

$$* \quad * \quad *$$

The Japanese do not encourage civilian flying, so you may encounter difficulty in getting permission to go there. However, assuming that the permission has been granted, there are several routes to Japan depending on the weather. One can go from one of the Aleutian Islands down to Japan, being extremely careful not to stray into Russian airspace. Or one can go direct from Wake Island up to Tokyo, which is a distance of 1770 nautical miles; or from Guam overhead Iwo Jima, which is 1380 nautical miles.

Tokyo is 35° North latitude so we get back into the Temperate Zone of prevailing Westerlies; it is also close to the Asian continent, so the weather bears a resemblance to that found off the East Coast of the American continent.

"DOWN UNDER" TO AUSTRALIA AND NEW ZEALAND

Believe it or not, the distance to Sydney, Australia, or Auckland, New Zealand, from San Francisco is a wee bit shorter than the distance from San Francisco to Manila in the Philippines. I think it sounds longer because it is in the Southern Hemisphere.

When we leave either Honolulu or Hilo for Australia, we have some choice of routes, depending on our fuel range and which islands we are interested in seeing. For pilots who are delivering an airplane on a fixed-price contract the best way is from Hilo down to Pago Pago in American Samoa; fuel here is less than one-half as much as it is in Tarawa and some of the other islands. Airport fees are also much cheaper. However, it is the longest distance, being 2200 nautical miles from Hilo and 2300 from Honolulu in a straight line. The Hawaiian chain of Loran stations is useful for 500 to 600 nautical miles, but from there you are on your own as there are no Loran stations South of the equator. For this reason I have preferred to go from Honolulu down to Canton Island, which has a strong NDB; this adds 75 miles to the straight-line distance but it gives me a spot of definite position. I do like to know where I am now and then.

FIGURE 11-8

After an all-night flight from Hawaii one welcomes the sight of the mountains of Tutuila Island in American Samoa. One or two hours after sunrise is the best time to arrive.

Pago Pago (pronounced "Pango Pango") is the principal town on the island of Tutuila in American Samoa. It lies 13 degrees south of the equator and is therefore very tropical. It is also very mountainous (Figure 11-8); so much so that in order to have an airport the runway had to be built out into the bay (Figure 11-9). The harbor is reputed to be the best one in the South Pacific, and as such was used by whaling ships at the end of the last ·century. The whalers were shortly followed by New England missionaries so the islanders use a mixture of their own age-old religion and Christianity. They have resisted our custom of burying the dead in church cemeteries and cling to the old custom of burying the dead in their own front yards. This makes for interesting sights as you tour the island because for the first year after death the grave mound is kept gaily decorated with small flags, flowers and various tinselly things.

The island is worth at least a few days stay as the scenery is beautiful, and the people and their customs are interesting. Hotel accommodations range from very plush down to not very comfortable.

FIGURE 11-9
Because there is almost no flat land in Tutuila, the Pago Pago airport has been built out into the water.

From Pago Pago we can go to Noumea and on to Brisbane or Sydney, or we can go to Norfolk Island as long as it is not Tuesday, when Norfolk is closed. Remember that it is

Tuesday in Norfolk when it is Monday in Pago Pago. From Norfolk it is a short run over to Sydney. If New Zealand is our destination, the distance from Pago Pago to Auckland is 1565 miles.

For shorter legs we can go from Honolulu down over Johnston Island (Figure 11-10) to Majuro and from there to Honiara on Guadalcanal and on into Townsville, Australia. Another route is from Honolulu to Tarawa and from there down to Noumea, on the island of New Caledonia, and then on to Brisbane or Sydney.

A trip to Australia or New Zealand takes us from 20° North Latitude through the area of the Northeast Trade Winds down through the Doldrums which lie from 10 degrees North to 10 degrees South of the equator and on through the area of the Southeast Trade Winds and into the

FIGURE 11-10
Life on Johnston Island (720 nautical miles Southwest of Honolulu) is quite restricted. Here is practically the whole of the island. It's a military base, so don't land, but do talk to them.

Southern Temperate Zone, starting at 30° South Latitude. Tasmania and the South Island of New Zealand lie in the zone of the "Roaring Forties," where the wind becomes predominantly Westerly and brisk.

The "doldrums" are the home of that Intertropical Front we have mentioned; in the Northern summer the thunderstorms, if any, will be found chiefly in the 10 degrees North of the equator, and in the Southern summer they will be found in the 10 degrees below the equator. These are the "rainy seasons." A thunderstorm is a thunderstorm of course, but it is usually possible to avoid the ones in this area as they are not in a solid line (or seldom are). One wants to check the forecast and satellite pictures very carefully at each stop, but I know pilots who have never encountered any thunderstorms in many trips to Australia.

Once we get below 10° South Latitude we are reasonably safe from thunderstorms and the wind will again blow, this time from the Southeast as a norm. However, at the appropriate seasons, one must be as alert for typhoons (or hurricanes) in the South Pacific as one is in the North Pacific or the Atlantic. Darwin, Australia, was almost completely destroyed by one on Christmas of 1974, and New Caledonia has also suffered from hurricanes at times. The Trade Winds are usually light at 6000 to 8000 feet (about 10 to 15 knots), and in the equatorial area there are only vagrant breezes.

GENERAL INFORMATION

Except for the area between Wake or Guam and Japan all Variations in the Pacific are Easterly. This means that they must be subtracted from the *True* Heading in order to get a Magnetic Heading (see Chapters 6 and 9).

The route to Japan via the Aleutians requires Aircraft Position Chart 3094.

The route from San Francisco to Hawaii requires Aircraft Position Chart 3096.

The route from Hawaii to Manila via Wake and Guam requires Aircraft Position Chart 3087, which also goes up to Tokyo from Wake or Guam.

The route from Hawaii through Samoa to Australia and New Zealand requires Aircraft Position Chart 3088.

There is no Aircraft Position Chart which shows the islands of Majuro, Tarawa, Guadalcanal, or the others in that area, so you will also need Global Navigation Chart GNC 7.

Radio Facility Charts and Approach plates are also necessary and are available either from the Department of Commerce or from Jeppesen Company.

I think it is also well to carry World Aeronautical and Operational Navigation Charts for the land areas over which you will be flying.

Because of the distance involved in each 5 degrees longitude enroute from San Francisco to Honolulu or Hilo, Air Traffic Control wants a report every $2\frac{1}{2}$ degrees of longitude rather than every 5 degrees, as on the North Atlantic. They prefer to hear from us at least every hour.

West and South of Hawaii, every island requires prior permission for landing and fueling from the appropriate agency. North of the equator the islands are primarily American, and the appropriate agency is either the Navy or the Air Force. The fueling request is necessary because sometimes there is a shortage of one kind or another, mostly due to transportation problems, as I understand it. South of the equator the islands belong to Britain, France, Australia, New Zealand, etc., and permission must be obtained from their respective governments through Embassies or Consulates, which can also tell you about the fuel supplier.

In Europe we do not need visas in our passports, but in Africa, Asia, and Australia visas are necessary, so be prepared.

Flying over the Pacific is different from flying over the North Atlantic; the distances are much longer, and there is little airline traffic West and South of Hawaii, so there is nobody to talk to when you get lonesome. While the weather is usually good, when it is bad it is horrid. Practically every island has an NDB, but some of them are only turned on by request, so check the ones you plan to use. With careful preparation and plenty of patience to sit for a long time waiting for an island to show up, flying around the Pacific can be very interesting, particularly if you like warm to hot weather.

2 Foreign Governments

If we are crossing the North Atlantic to Europe, we will be guests of several governments and subject to their regulations; these are not onerous but are different in some respects from what we are used to at home.

VFR of course means flying by Visual Flight Rules and is predicated on navigating by pilotage with constant reference to the ground. Therefore, one cannot be VFR either when on top of clouds or at night because in either case one cannot see the ground. Other countries do not recognize VFR on top or at night for this reason. Airway floors are variable, depending on the underlying terrain, so that VFR beneath an airway is possible, and of course one can be VFR off airways. Oceanic controlled airspace starts at 5500 feet, so one can cross the ocean below that VFR and without communicating; however, I could not advise this for two reasons:

1. It will get lonesome with nobody to talk to and knowing that nobody knows or cares what happens to you until past your estimated time of arrival at destination.

2. It will not be easy to get back into the system for landing at destination if the weather is other than CAVOK, and the less good the weather the longer the delay you will have in getting landing clearance.

VFR flight plans are necessary even for a local flight and require a weather briefing before filing. This is for your own protection as much as anything, but is something you must get used to and comply with. Only in the United States and Canada can we jump in an airplane and go without saying aye, yes, or no to anyone; even in Canada a flight plan is necessary if going across any water or into a wilderness area away from civilization.

Over the ocean or above the *transition level* the altimeter is set to *standard pressure*, which is 29.92 inches or 1013.2 millibars. Transition level, as the name implies, is the altitude at which we switch from local pressure to standard; it is usually between 4000 and 5500 feet above sea level, depending on the terrain and the local pressure. In mountainous areas it will be higher, naturally.

While there are many VORs in use in other countries, the airways depend as much, and in some places more, on NDBs. The wind does not always blow along an airway, so being able to fly an NDB with a crosswind is important; we discussed this procedure in Chapter 9, Navigation.

Compulsory reporting points over the ocean are every 5 degrees of longitude for airplanes cruising less than 300 knots and every 10 degrees of longitude for the faster airplanes; additionally one must report when entering the airspace of another controlling agency, whether over the ocean or on an airway. In Europe this sometimes means a report every 4 or 5 minutes.

PAPERS FOR THE AIRPLANE

Certain papers must be in the airplane at all times, others are required only in certain locations or under certain circumstances.

Required	Where applicable
Registration Certificate	Ferry Permit
Airworthiness Certificate	FAA Form 337
Aircraft Log Book	Overflight Permits
Engine Log Book(s)	Landing Permits
Certificate of Insurance	Military Permits
General Declarations	

Registration and Airworthiness Certificates must be in the airplane at all times, and occasionally you will have to go back to where it is parked if an official wants to see them.

Log books for both aircraft and engine(s) must be in the airplane at all times, but it is wise to carry them with you when going to the Immigration authorities in any country as they frequently want to see and stamp them. In other countries it is necessary that each book be filled in completely, with an entry in every column, and signed by the pilot. The record must be clear as to origin and destination of the flight, time enroute, passengers' names, and any mechanical remarks which are appropriate. With one engine you will have two books to fill in and with two engines, three books. Each book must be brought up to date after every flight and always available for inspection.

You will need a Certificate of Insurance from your insurance company affirming that you have adequate Liability coverage for any accident in which you might be involved. This certificate must also be readily available for inspection by the local authorities.

If you have installed long-range tanks, it is wise to have the Ferry Permit and the FAA Form 337 available in case someone wants to see it.

Permission for overflight and landing permissions are needed if you plan to go to any country other than the European ones. In Africa, the Middle East, Asia, the Philippines, and Japan these permits are absolutely required; they will take from 2 to several weeks to obtain, so start early. Eastern Europe behind the Iron Curtain also requires them.

In the Pacific North of the equator we are in United States territory and must deal with the military, as explained in Chapter 10 and 11. The Philippines, Japan, and all the islands south of the equator except American Samoa are foreign and require the same paperwork as the countries around the North Atlantic. These islands belong to Britain, France, New Zealand, and Australia so they are all friendly, and the chief reason for the prior permission is to be sure that there is fuel available. Fuel all comes by tanker, and it has happened that typhoons or other phenomena of Nature have prevented the tankers from docking or unloading, so that the island is out of fuel and we must go to another. Also Norfolk Island is closed on Tuesday, and some others have their days as well.

PAPERS FOR THE CREW

The crew must carry certain required papers, with other required only in certain locations.

Required	Where applicable
Pilot License	Visas
Current Medical Certificate	Record of Shots
Pilot Log Book	
Passports	
General Declarations	

Pilot License and Medical are of course necessary.

Pilot Log Book must be available and up to date for inspection by the authorities; actually it is seldom asked for, but when it is. . . .

In Europe a passport is enough, and one does not need a visa; but in any other area—in Africa, the Middle East, Asia, Japan, the Phillippines, and Australia—one must have a visa. It can be obtained either in person or by mail from any Consulate of the country to which you wish to go.

Vaccinations, including small pox, cholera, yellow fever, typhoid, and tetanus, may be necessary and are probably desirable if you are planning to go to any country outside Europe.

General Declarations belong in both the Airplane and Crew papers. Figure 12-1 is a typical General Declaration (otherwise known as Gen Dec), which must be filled out more or less as shown. It is a good idea to take some extra blank ones with you as many countries like to see their name at the top instead of down in the "Place" column. If there are not more than three persons on board, it is sometimes cheaper to list them all as crew rather than passengers because there are countries which will charge for passengers or otherwise make things more difficult for them. Some places you will need three or four of these forms and some places none, but I always have two available for each stop I will make, just to save time.

*   *   *

Governments change or sometimes change their regulations. These statements are applicable in 1978, but it is always well to check the International Flight Information Manual for any changes in requirements or regulations which could affect your flight.

FIGURE 12-1

General Declaration form, showing side to be filled in.

Customs Form 7507
THE DEPARTMENT OF THE TREASURY
6.7, 6.8, 6.9,C. R.
March 1969

Form Approved.
Budget Bureau No. 48-R0153

GENERAL DECLARATION

(Outward/Inward)

AGRICULTURE, CUSTOMS, IMMIGRATION, AND PUBLIC HEALTH

Owner or Operator ..... *JOHN JONES*

Marks of Nationality and Registration 1) *USA   N1234Z* Flight No. *PVT*   Date *6/10/78*

Departure from ..... *BANGOR, ME.* (Place)   Arrival at ..... *PRESTWICK* (Place)

FLIGHT ROUTING

("Place" Column always to list origin, every en-route stop and destination)

PLACE	TOTAL NUMBER OF CREW 1)	NUMBER OF PASSENGERS ON THIS STAGE 2)
FT. CHIMO	*JOHN JONES*	
FROBISHER	*FRED SMITH*	
SONDRESTROM	*MARY SMITH*	**Departure Place:** *0*
REYKJAVIK		Embarking ....
		Through on same flight ....
		Arrival Place: *0*
		Disembarking ....
		Through on same flight ....

Declaration of Health

Persons on board known to be suffering from illness other than airsickness or the effects of accidents, as well as those cases of illness disembarked during the flight:

Any other condition on board which may lead to the spread of disease:

Details of each disinsecting or sanitary treatment (place, date, time, method) during the flight. If no disinsecting has been carried out during the flight give details of most recent disinsecting:

Signed, if required ....
Crew Member Concerned

For official use only

I declare that all statements and particulars contained in this General Declaration, and in any supplementary forms required to be presented with this General Declaration are complete, exact and true to the best of my knowledge and that all through passengers will continue/have continued on the flight.

SIGNATURE *John Jones*
Authorized Agent or Pilot-in-Command

1) To be completed only when required by the State.
2) Not to be completed when passenger manifests are presented and to be completed only when required by the State.

FUEL TAXES

Like us in the United States, citizens of every country must pay taxes on their fuel, and in many countries these taxes are as much as 50 percent of the total price.

Unlike the United States, most countries are kind to people flying to and through their countries, so if the airplane is leaving the country and will therefore use the fuel in another country the tax will not be collected from the purchaser. Usually this is accomplished by the purchaser signing a Customs form or "drawback" to assure a refund if the fuel was paid for with cash, or the oil company is advised and the bill received is minus the tax if we are using an International Carnet, which is the only credit card usable for fuel in foreign countries. Both Shell and Esso will issue these Carnets to their customers if asked before starting the trip. In the last few years a few countries are refusing to accept a Carnet, but on the whole it saves time and frustration in getting money exchanged to the local currency to buy fuel. With a fuel Carnet and an internationally recognized credit card, like Diner's Club or American Express, one need not carry so much cash, and there are pickpockets all over the world. A friend of mine who is a ferry pilot had his pocket picked recently at Heathrow Airport to the tune of $700.

In Europe airplane owners try when possible to fill their tanks in a neighboring country; since everybody in all countries does it, probably each country comes out about the same in fuel-tax collection.

COMMUNICATION/NAVIGATION
CHARGES ON BOTH OCEANS

International pilots must plan in trip budgets for charges for both communication and navigation services, even if they are not used for whatever reason. Canada levies a charge of $30 Canadian for Telecommunications and $50 Canadian for Enroute Facilities. A few years ago the Canadian controllers had a strike; all flying had to be VFR; there was no communication possible, but the communication bill arrived on schedule. I protested that it was bad enough to have to pay to talk to them because they wanted me to but was adding insult to injury to bill me for talking when there was nobody to talk to! This netted me nothing and I had to pay it.

Shannon levies a charge of £9, which works out to about $17 more or less, depending on the rate of exchange at the time of the bill; this charge is for "contact," which I presume is communications.

Iceland and Denmark put their heads together and decided to get their share of the "pound of flesh." If you cross the North Atlantic at any latitude above 40° North you must pay these two governments £13.5, which means approximately $25.

If I am going "North about" through Greenland and Iceland, this seems not unfair in view of everybody else's charges; I am after all using their facilities. However, on the Gander to Shannon route which is from 50 to 53° North and well into their zone of charging, I do resent it because the distance is too great to use either navigation or communication facilities. For a year I argued with both Iceland and Denmark and letters flew (from the time it took to get an answer, I rather think the letters paddled) back and forth. By the end of the year I had quite a stack of bills, but again it netted me nothing. Iceland was polite but firm and Denmark was insulting and firm: I had to pay the charges.

If your destination is Scotland, they get in their licks and charge for navigation to find the airport.

From the time you arrive in Iceland you are in Europe, and here we have Eurocontrol, which bills for all the countries whose airways you are using. These charges vary with each segment of airway and with each landfall airport. Also the charges increase rather dramatically every few months, so an estimate is quite impossible. As an indication, a recent trip from Shannon to Munich cost $83 and from Reykjavik to Munich cost $120. Fortunately for single-engine owners, so far Eurocontrol charges only twin-engine airplanes for use of the airways.

You do not escape by going to Santa Maria because Eurocontrol takes care of the charges through the Azores.

All these charges are unavoidable because your name and address are on file as soon as you make your first position report (each control area requests it on the first call-up); the bills will arrive soon after you return home.

If we add up all the charges for enroute and the high landing fees at every airport, plus the cost of fuel and tie-down, it is easy to see why general aviation in Europe is not as flourishing as ours.

ριοſtſcript

If you are still with me in these final pages, dear reader, you will have discovered not only that ocean flying can be fascinating but also that the knowledge required which differs from that needed in domestic flying is not onerous but rather a delightful challenge for which the rewards will be great and lasting.

Even your domestic flying must improve because of:

1. The greater care demanded by the airplane, its engine, and accessories;

2. The increased knowledge of navigation and wind triangles, drift correction, ADF tracking, *True* and Magnetic Courses and Headings, etc.

3. The ability to get more accurate weather information.

Rarely will you be alone in your crossing; hundreds of United States built airplanes are delivered under their own power to all the countries of the free world every year because this is the cheapest, safest, and quickest way of getting them to their new owners. Only the smallest and slowest are crated and shipped. At any given moment you can meet one or more of the 75 or so ferry pilots engaged in delivering these airplanes, so the oceans are not really lonesome expanses. Controllers and forecasters are also helpful if asked.

Certainly it is not as cheap to fly your own airplane across as it is to go with the airlines; but how many of us use the bus in preference to our own cars for a vacation trip? Or a business trip?

Whether flying a corporate jet or a four-place single-engine airplane, one sees more of the world than is possible in an airliner.

Also consider the advantages on arrival at any airport. As an airline passenger we are herded through Immigration and Customs like cattle. If we are in our own airplane, we use the crew entrance and Immigration and Customs see us as people. (If you are a woman they may have difficulty believing that you came across the ocean without a *man pilot!*)

Our baggage will not get lost, and we avoid the mob scene around the baggage carousel waiting for it to show up (or not to show up because it went someplace else).

True it is that the general aviation airplane is parked as far away from the terminal as the ramp allows, but almost every airport sends out a ramp attendant with transportation who will take you to the Crew entrance. Madrid is an exception; once I arrived there in the pouring rain (very unusual they claim) and was directed by Ground Control to park more than half a mile away. Nobody came out, so I sat in the airplane until a guard truck approached; I flashed my landing light in his eyes until he came over to see what was going on, and with sign language I persuaded him to take me to the terminal.

English is the Aviation language as long as you are in the air, although sometimes you must listen closely to be sure.

Once on the ground, a few words of the local language helps the sign language in getting fuel or whatever else you need.

More and more pilots are flying their own planes across the oceans of the world for business or pleasure or ferrying planes across to earn a living. If this book helps to make the trip enjoyable and uneventful, my purpose in writing it has been fulfilled.

Ten Commandments of Ocean Flying

    I. Thou shalt be careful in the getting of thy Weather Briefing.

    II. Thou shalt not ignore the wind; it will take revenge on thee.

    III. Thou shalt not leave behind the tools of thy trade: Aircraft Position Chart, dividers, computer, plotter, flight-plan form, straightedge, pencil.

    IV. Thou shalt be accurate in the working of thy wind triangle.

    V. Thou shalt not confuse thy Course with thy Heading.

    VI. Thou shalt not confuse *True* with Magnetic.

    VII. Thou shalt remember that thy *True* Course will be thy Track if thou didst thy wind triangles correctly.

    VIII. Thou shalt be careful with Variation; applied in the wrong direction, it can lead thee to uninhabited areas.

    IX. Thou shalt be accurate in the holding of thy Headings.

    X. Thou shalt learn to track a straight line with thy ADF in crosswinds.

Letter Identifiers
for Aerodromes

International flight plans require four-letter identifiers for aerodromes. Except for the United States, Canada, Australia, and Micronesia, which can be identified by their first letter, countries can be identified by the second letter of this identifier. The last two letters indicate the aerodrome but are not always easy to guess.

Australia	A___	AMML = Melbourne
Canada	C___	CYQX = Gander
Micronesia	P___	PGUM = Agana, Guam
United States	K___	KBOS = Boston

In the North Atlantic

Greenland	BG__	BGSF = Sondrestrom
Iceland	BI__	BIRK = Reykjavik

In Europe

Belgium	EB__	EBBR = Brussels
España	EC__	ECMD = Madrid
Deutschland	ED__	EDDM = Munich
Finland	EF__	EFHK = Helsinki (Vantaa)
Great Britain	EG__	EGPK = Prestwick
Holland	EH__	EHAM = Amsterdam
Ireland	EI__	EINN = Shannon
Denmark	EK__	EKYT = Aalborg
Norway	EN__	ENFB = Oslo
Sweden	ES__	ESSA = Stockholm (Arlanda)
France	LF__	LFPO = Paris (Orly)
Italy	LI__	LIBB = Brindisi
Österreich	LO__	LOWW = Wien (Schwechat) Vienna, Austria
Portugal and Azores	LP__	LPAZ = Santa Maria LPPT = Lisbon
Switzerland	LS__	LSZH = Zurich (Kloten)

In the Pacific

Fiji	NF__	NFFN = Nandi
Samoa (American)	NS__	NSTU = Pago Pago
New Zealand	NZ__	NZCH = Christchurch
Japan	RJ__	RJOO = Osaka
Philippines	RP__	RPMM = Manila

VOR-TACAN Frequency Conversions

Through trial and error I have determined that I can receive the listed TACAN channels on my DME when its VOR/DME receiver is tuned to the apposite VOR frequency.

VOR frequency	TACAN channel	VOR frequency	TACAN channel
108.4	21	113.6	83
108.6	23	114.0	87
108.8	25	114.3	90
109.0	27	114.6	93
109.4	31	114.9	96
109.8	35	115.0	97
110.2	39	115.3	100
110.6	43	115.6	103
111.0	47	115.9	106
111.4	51	116.0	107
111.8	55	116.4	111
112.0	57	116.6	113
112.4	71	116.9	116
112.7	74	117.0	117
112.9	76	117.4	121
113.1	78	117.6	123
113.3	80	117.9	126

Index